ONE

BY

ONE

• • •

WELCOMING THE SINGLES
IN YOUR CHURCH

GINA DALFONZO

BakerBooks
a division of Baker Publishing Group
Grand Rapids, Michigan

Published by Baker Books
a division of Baker Publishing Group
P.O. Box 6287, Grand Rapids, MI 49516-6287
www.bakerbooks.com

Printed in the United States of America

Library of Congress Cataloging-in-Publication Data
Names: Dalfonzo, Gina, 1975–
Title: One by one : welcoming the singles in your church / Gina Dalfonzo.
Description: Grand Rapids, MI : Baker Books, 2017. | Includes bibliographical
    references.
Identifiers: LCCN 2016059367 | ISBN 9780801072932 (pbk.)
Subjects: LCSH: Church work with single people. | Single people—Religious life.
Classification: LCC BV639.S5 D35 2017 | DDC 259.086/52—dc23
LC record available at https://lccn.loc.gov/2016059367

In keeping with biblical principles of creation stewardship, Baker Publishing Group advocates the responsible use of our natural resources. As a member of the Green Press Initiative, our company uses recycled paper when possible. The text paper of this book is composed in part of post-consumer waste.

17 18 19 20 21 22 23   7 6 5 4 3 2 1

"Here's a book on singleness that won't tell you how to score a spouse nor condemn a growing generation of unmarried Christians. Instead, Gina Dalfonzo shares her own story along with many others', enriching our understanding of the stereotypes they face and the faith they live by."

Kate Shellnutt, *Christianity Today*

"Many of our churches continue to focus their outreach and programming toward families, often (unintentionally) leaving Christian singles feeling as though they're on the outside looking in. Gina Dalfonzo offers an insight-filled and gracious look at the ways in which both individual congregations and Christian subculture haven't been especially hospitable to singles. In addition, she offers readers thoughtful ways in which they can include, enfold, and honor the experiences of singles in their churches. *One by One* is full of practical wisdom that a congregation of any size can use to create a culture of welcome for every member of the body of Christ."

Michelle Van Loon, author of *Moments & Days: How Our Holy Celebrations Shape Our Faith*

"Without preaching or shaming, Gina Dalfonzo tells the church what we need to know: that is, the experience of the singles in our midst (or, perhaps of the singles who can't stand to be in it!). With sometimes hilarious and always warm and wise insights from her life, as well as the lives of other single people, Dalfonzo shows us ways to fully love and welcome our single brothers and sisters."

Caryn Rivadeneira, author of *Known and Loved: 52 Devotions from the Psalms*

"*One by One* is a desperately needed book just now for churches serious about honoring the inherent dignity of all who enter their doors. In this very practical book, Gina identifies how the church underserves singles even while the larger culture leaves them looking for connection and truth. I hope it gets the wide reading it deserves."

John Stonestreet, president, the Chuck Colson Center for Christian Worldview

"*One by One* is an immensely insightful encouragement to every churchgoer. The book is beautifully written and brimming with stories and hard-won wisdom. Gina Dalfonzo encourages us to not only love the singles in our midst but to also empower them, tapping into an amazing resource for the kingdom. A thoroughly enjoyable read!"

Mary DeMuth, author of *Worth Living: How God's Wild Love for You Makes You Worthy*

"When it comes to singles in the church, this is the book the evangelical church has needed! Dalfonzo makes fair critiques while also expressing gratitude for the church. And then she graciously offers a way forward. This book is smart, persuasive, and convicting. I want to hand a copy to every church leader I know. Dalfonzo is a wise and desperately needed voice in the evangelical church today. Heed her wisdom."

Marlena Graves, author of *A Beautiful Disaster*

"Intimate and excessively readable, Dalfonzo claims a spot for singles in every congregation in a voice at once both erudite and empathetic. Her pragmatic and compassionate tone, integrated with several perspectives from singles across the country, provides an integral space for acceptance and commonality. Essential reading for every member of a church congregation, *One by One* extends beyond the single experience and speaks to the church community at large."

Rachel McMillan, author of *A Lesson in Love and Murder*

"Gina Dalfonzo has written an important, wise, nuanced, and insightful book on singleness in the church. Weaving literary examples with interviews and Scripture, Gina has something to challenge and encourage all of us, single or married, pastor or layperson. As our culture's sexual ethics continue to move away from biblical standards, we will need voices like Dalfonzo's to articulate a virtuous, flourishing vision for singleness."

Alan Noble, PhD, editor-in-chief, *Christ and Pop Culture*

"Dalfonzo seeks to break down some of the stereotypes about Christian singles and change the way the church thinks about and interacts with the singles sitting beside them in the pews. Singles, like married couples and families, need support, sympathy, and celebration for important life events. Church leaders often don't realize this—which is why every pastor should have a copy of *One by One* on his or her desk."

Anne Morse, coauthor of *My Final Word* with Chuck Colson and *Prisoner of Conscience: One Man's Fight for Human and Religious Rights* with Frank Wolf

CONTENTS

Contents

A NOTE ABOUT THE INTERVIEWS IN THIS BOOK

To provide a range of perspectives on being a single Christian beyond just my own, I sent out a number of questionnaires to single friends and acquaintances who had agreed to share their thoughts and feelings on the subject of singleness. These interviewees represent a wide range of ages, ethnicities, backgrounds, and denominations. Names have been changed where requested. I have italicized all quotations from these interviewees to make it as easy as possible to distinguish their words from other quotations in this book.

These interviews were conducted over a number of years, as I worked on the book. Since being interviewed, some of the participants have married, but a number of them are still single. Regardless of their current marital status, all of them have had experience with prolonged singleness and had good, thoughtful insights to share. I'd like to thank them for their help.

ACKNOWLEDGMENTS

Thanks to my agent, Chris Park, for your unfailing support, wisdom, and guidance. Thanks to Bob Hosack, Lindsey Spoolstra, Patti Brinks, Abby Van Wormer, and the rest of the team at Baker Books for your insight, creativity, and hard work. I'm so grateful for all you've done.

Thanks to the OKJFC group, especially Dale Hanson Bourke and Katherine Willis Pershey, for helping me come up with a title for this book! Thank you to all my writing friends for your encouragement. I wish I had room to thank each one of you personally, but please know how much I appreciate you.

I owe a shout-out to Barnabas Piper, whose excellent book *The Pastor's Kid* helped me come up with the format and structure for this book. And I owe a debt of thanks to Turner Classic Movies for keeping me company during the long afternoons and late nights of writing, and to Juan Diego Flórez, Mariusz Kwiecień, and Anna Netrebko for making the music that pulled me across the finish line. Never underestimate the power of good music and good movies!

Thanks to Wendy Bilen, Martha Anderson, Kim Moreland, Annie Provencher, and Mary Ann Compher for friendship, support, and feedback. Thanks to Pastor Johnny Kurcina and the Extended Family small group at Christ Church Vienna for modeling how the church can learn to consider, listen to, and include single people.

Thanks to Lucia D'alfonso for helping so much with the family research. Thanks to Rachel McMillan and Ruth Anderson—I could not have done this without you.

Thanks to Laura van der Goes-Lim for your friendship and encouragement and for sharing your family with me—I cannot imagine a more valuable gift. Thank you to Lydia, Anna, and Ezra for the joy and inspiration you give me.

Thanks to my grandparents for the wonderful memories you left me. I hold you in my heart. Thank you to Joy Dalfonzo for always believing in me—I couldn't ask for a more supportive, caring sister.

Thank you, Mom and Dad, for everything. I mean *everything*. I could thank you all day, every day, for the rest of my life and it still wouldn't be enough.

Thanks most of all to Jesus Christ, my Lord, my Savior, and my Rock. In You is life.

INTRODUCTION

"Do you have children?" asked the nice lady in the church restroom after I had introduced myself.

"No," I replied, and added, "I'm not married."

Sudden, awkward silence.

This little dialogue—what there was of it—will be instantly recognizable to most single Christians. To announce your singleness is very often the way to bring a conversation with a fellow churchgoer to a screeching halt.

Here's a commenter called "Daisy" at the *Wartburg Watch* blog:

> If you . . . when asked (even at church or church functions), "Are you married/ have kids?" . . . say "No, never" the person gets quiet real fast and doesn't know how to talk to you after. You're made to feel like a freak.[1]

And here's a story from my friend Fiona:

> *The last women's retreat I attended had an icebreaker activity the first night. Every question assumed that women were married with children and did not work*

outside the home. One of the icebreakers was "If you have more than three children, move to the table behind you and get to know others at that table." A young woman came to my table, and her first question was "Well, how many children do you have?" When I replied, "I don't have any children. I've never been married," she said in a pitying voice, "Oh!" and with a stricken look on her face shrank back in her chair in silence.

To understand the experiences of Daisy, Fiona, myself, and many, many others, you have to understand that today's church—particularly the evangelical Protestant church—sees itself as deeply, irrevocably family-oriented. At a time when divorce, cohabitation, and teen pregnancy are rampant, the church has taken its stand in favor of doing things the biblical way: married parents raising children in the fear and admonition of the Lord.

It naturally follows that families, especially families with children, are honored, encouraged, supported, and praised by the church. And that's a good thing. Parents of young children are doing a tough and often thankless job; I've taken care of enough children in my life, even though only temporarily, to know that. They need all the encouragement and support they can get.

What the church doesn't always understand is that single Christians need encouragement and support too.

On the Margins

I do not feel that the church has been supportive of me as a single. I have had pastors, elders, and their wives say to me that [my church] is not a good church for older singles. ("Why do you attend here?")—Erin

I think that churches don't know how to minister to singles—because protracted singleness is such a new phenomenon and so many churches are trapped in wishing that it was still the 1950s.—Ashley

A single stands out as apart from the crowd, and not in a positive way. There are no invitations to lunch after church or other social gatherings, mainly because I don't really "fit in."—Jim

I think nowadays the church has put so much focus on the nuclear family (especially ones with children) that anything other than that gets pushed to the wayside.—Robyn

Frankly, a lot of the time, the church simply doesn't know what to do with the single and childless. We haven't followed the standard path. Marriage seminars and couples' weekends are not for us. There aren't a lot of sermons about how we should navigate our lives and relationships—and when there are, as my friend Eric once remarked, they usually boil down to "Don't have sex."

We don't have children in AWANA and Sunday school. The ushers aren't supposed to hand us roses on Mother's Day. We can't talk diapers and homework and lost retainers and three a.m. feedings. (Well, we can, if we have extensive experience with friends' babies and young relatives, or even if we remember some of our own childhood experiences. But honestly, most people don't expect or want us to have much to say. Why hear from the dilettante when you can go straight to the experts?)

And seeing as how most of us have never had the chance to practice the daily, selfless love that having our own family requires, we *must* be arrogant and self-centered, as well as ignorant about all these really important things in life. It stands to reason.

Not only that, but we're living, breathing contradictions of certain teachings that have become pervasive in the evangelical church. Generations of young churchgoers have been taught that if they just stay abstinent until marriage, if they properly practice dating or, more often, courtship, they'll be blessed with great, sexually fulfilling marriages.

But what of those of us who did follow the rules and have remained single into our thirties, forties, and fifties? We're the bad examples, the anomalies, the ones you *don't* want to teach the kids about . . . even if we did everything right. Who wants to stand up in front of a Sunday school class or youth conference and say, "Be abstinent until you get married—and oh, by the way, it's possible you'll never get married"?

The head of the organization I work for, John Stonestreet, knows something about this unenviable task. John frequently speaks to Christian homeschool groups, and when he does, he sometimes quotes from an article I wrote about "princess theology" (the teachings about how "you're a princess and God will bring you a knight" that are so popular with many Christian educators).[2] John sets out to disillusion his young listeners gently about those princesses and knights. He breaks it to them that, in fact, following a specific formula does not necessarily mean God will give them a spouse.

John tells me that many of these students, especially the girls, get really upset over this. This is not what they've been taught, and it's definitely not what they want to hear. I feel sorry for those kids, but I'd feel even sorrier if they were to keep believing that lie and then blame God for not making their dreams come true. Or if they committed to chastity unaware of what it might require of them and then ended up walking away from their faith altogether when that commitment required more than they believed they could handle, as so many have done.

I've actually asked a few Christians to try to imagine going fifty-two years without sex. The look I get is pretty interesting.—Carole

As I was working on this book, a story broke on social media about Christian football player and abstinence advocate Tim Tebow getting dumped by his girlfriend over "lack of sex." Who knows how accurate it was—probably as accurate as any given trending headline on Facebook, which is to say, maybe possibly a tiny bit accurate (but not much). The point is, as one might expect in this day and age, the internet was soon overrun with mockery of Tebow and his beliefs.

For about half a second, I thought of sending him a "Good for you" message, just to counter it all. Then I thought better of it—not just because my one puny message would most likely get lost in the social media flood but also because a young man who's dedicated to chastity probably does not want to hear "Good for you" from a forty-year-old celibate woman. It'd be like getting a "Welcome to the Lonely Hearts Club" letter from Miss Havisham. However faithful and devout Tim Tebow is, it's safe to say that I am the person he does *not* want to become.

And yet, somehow, we anomalies are fast becoming the norm. Many people have tried to figure out why. The problem is that even when their intentions are good their understanding is often incomplete.

An Insider's View

Some women have occasionally alluded to the fact that I spent a lot of time pursuing my career/education, and that might have affected why I am still single. I understand the point somewhat, but I despise it when it is cast in a certain tone. If I happened to meet the right man while I was in the process of all these things, I would have certainly wanted to marry him. Should I have sat around and not pursued these things and waited for marriage to happen instead?—Bea

In June 2010, sociologist W. Bradford Wilcox stated in an interview, "I think the emergence of a 'soulmate' model of marriage, where young men and women hold very high expectations for a future spouse, helps to explain why more women—especially highly educated women—find themselves without a husband and a desire to have a child as their biological clock winds down."[3]

The important thing to remember here is that Wilcox is a sociologist. It's his job to look at the statistics on a given issue and try to identify and analyze trends. He's actually a very good sociologist; several years ago he wrote a book called *Soft Patriarchs, New Men* about certain trends and behaviors among Christian husbands and fathers that I thought was excellent, and I've followed his work ever since.

But sociology has limits. It can see numbers but it can't really see the people behind them. And I believe that, in an area as complex and sensitive as this, sociology can't necessarily capture all the reasons behind a trend. As a result, there are times when it paints these trends with too broad a brush.

That's why we single people have grown used to hearing statisticians and sociologists make pronouncements about us that have very little to do with our actual experience. While a sociologist might look at educated single women and see a group that tends to be too picky, the truth is "high expectations" can mean simply "the hope of finding a guy with whom one can begin and maintain a conversation lasting longer than ten minutes, let alone a relationship." And I'm not male-bashing here; a lot of single Christian men have similar things to say about the women they've dated.

In short, sometimes people get caught up in trends when they never wanted to. Personally, I was absolutely certain, from the time I was about five years old, that someday I would be married and have children. It never occurred to me to doubt it. Of course, I also thought I was going to be a ballerina *and* a concert pianist, so my dreams weren't always realistic. But the dream of marriage and a family—that one seemed like a reasonable and easily reachable goal. It happened to almost everyone, after all.

Fast-forward three decades.

When I turned thirty-five and was still single, I felt a little like Roxie Hart in the musical *Chicago*. I admit that's not a very sanctified reference (and I should probably specify that I didn't actually want to shoot anyone), but it's one I couldn't seem to stop thinking about. Like Roxie, I was older than I had ever intended to be—at least, while still being single—and facing "one big world full of no."

I hadn't deliberately delayed marriage; on the contrary, I had eagerly hoped and prayed for it. I had done my educational and career planning—my real career planning, I mean, beyond the ballerina-and-pianist stage—with that goal in mind: I wanted to be a writer, not just because I loved to write but also because it could fit well with being a stay-at-home mom. And I'd gone out with a number of Christian men, looking for the one God might have for me.

But for some reason, none of those relationships ever really went anywhere. Marriage, despite my certainty that it was my destiny, just did not happen. And it's the same story for many of my friends—and for many beyond my circle of friends as well.

Here are just a few of the explanations that frequently get tossed around: (1) There are more Christian women than men. (2) Christian relationship fads have swept through the church, leaving both sexes afraid to talk to each other. (3) Too many singles are content with their status. (4) There are too many small groups or not enough small groups. (5) There is too much "being friends" or not enough "being friends" . . . the list of explanations goes on and on and on. Some have validity, others not so much. But regardless, it seems that a new one pops up with every day that passes.

It all boils down to this: so many of us who desire marriage and children simply don't manage to get there. In all honesty, the fads, trends, and "how to" books just haven't done us that much good. In fact, many of them have left us feeling more helpless, alone, and unequipped to deal with the opposite sex than we were before. And they've left the rest of the church wondering what on earth went wrong and how to fix it.

This book attempts to deal with some of the difficult questions and issues raised by this unprecedented situation.

But before we get underway, here's what this book is *not*. It's not a place for me to try to provide everyone with answers and solutions and The One Best Way to Snag a Spouse. (If I knew that, I'd already be married and I wouldn't be writing this in the first place!) It's not a place for me to push a certain spiritual method of approaching singleness and marriage. It's not an attempt to try to revolutionize the church in some way; I'm more interested in trying to help create a better climate within the church than in trying to give the whole church a makeover.

This book is an insider's view. It goes behind the scenes, beneath the sociological and theological explanations, and explores some of what's really going on with single Christians.

As well, this book is meant to serve as a sort of mirror to the church, a way for a few of us single Christians to tell the church as a whole about the messages we've been hearing and what we think about those messages. It's a way for us to tell our fellow Christians about what our real needs and desires are and how the church can help support us in reaching our goals, living our lives for Christ, and becoming fully functioning, supportive members of the church. At the same time, it's also a way to discuss and to praise what the church is already doing well.

◆ ◆ ◆

My approach here, as I've hinted, is not a statistical one. The statistics on singleness have been covered and rehashed and analyzed elsewhere, by people who understand them much better than I do. I'll touch on them now and again, but more often, I'm simply going to share some of my own thoughts on the situation, along with the thoughts of various Christian single friends and friends of friends with whom I communicated while writing (as mentioned earlier), and the insights of single Christian writers and leaders whose works I've found helpful.

I hope these thoughts are useful and constructive. And I hope they start to break down some of the stereotypes and help change the way the church thinks about the singles in its midst. Church conversations like the one I described at the beginning could go very differently—and friendships between marrieds and singles in the church could grow and thrive—if we could learn to focus on the truth that a person's identity is found in Christ, not in his or her marital status. I hope this book will help with that process.

Two notes before we start. First, you'll find that I mostly focus on Christians who have been single all their lives. There's a reason for that—namely, that I'm part of that group. This is what I know best and what I'm best equipped to write about. I will incorporate the insights of divorcées and widows I've talked to and whose works I've read, where appropriate. But obviously, their experiences are something I cannot write about firsthand.

As one of my interviewees, Carole, put it:

Even among singles there are differences and differ-ent needs. A single/never married/no kids has different needs than one who has been married and may or may not have kids. A single mom has other needs.

> *It has been my experience that the church has improved on meeting the needs of single moms. Society has as well. But I feel like I don't fit at all.*

While acknowledging that the various groups among singles do indeed have different needs that should be addressed, I will keep my focus on the needs with which I'm most familiar. That said, the widowed and divorced are more than welcome to respond to this book with their own perspectives. I sincerely hope they do.

Second, throughout this book I will be talking about and quoting some prominent Christian thinkers, writers, and publications. I want to make it clear that, when pointing out the flaws in a quote or an argument, I'm not trying to judge or condemn the person or the publication as a whole. No matter how great or good a Christian may be, he or she is still human and therefore prone to mistakes—and nowadays, this particular subject seems to be hard for people to grasp clearly, making it especially likely to trip up even many good and smart Christians. So my deconstruction of some faulty thinking among our leaders is not meant to insult or demean them in any way. We all have our blind spots, myself included, and I will do my best here to treat others as I hope to be treated when my own errors are pointed out—with respect, humility, and grace.

Stigmas, Stereotypes, and Shame

What did I do wrong?

I look around me at family members, neighbors, colleagues. So many couples, so many families. So many people preoccupied with home and children and all the cares and concerns and mess and busyness and affection that go with them. So many people who have what I've been longing for . . . what I may never have.

Did I Do Something Wrong?

Having bought a subscription to Ancestry.com, I work on my family tree, tracing various branches further and further back, fascinated by the names and lives of people I've never known whose blood runs in my veins. Natalina married Giuseppe; their daughter Antonia married Luigi and then they Americanized their names to Antoinette and Louis (They really did! Maybe whoever was working at Ellis Island that day was a student of French history?); their son Albert married Martha; their daughter Joyce married Joe (son of Mary and Tony, grandson of Marco and Nicolina), and they became my parents.

And then there's me—still sitting there alone on my branch, feeling like I'm getting the ghostly side-eye from all those old Italians who married young and had lots of children and couldn't imagine how there could be any difficulty about the matter.

They tell me the Chinese have a name for people in my situation: "broken branches." "They are the biological dead ends of their family," explains journalist Mei Fong.[1] Am I a broken branch, a dead end? Will I be the end of that long line that was flourishing until I came along?

Why am I different? What did I do wrong?

These questions haunt many of us. In a sea of couples, we feel—pardon the pun—singled out, different, penalized for something we had so little control over. What *did* we do wrong? How could we have done things differently? How could we have made them go right?

"You Have Not Sinned"

Before we go any further, I need to make something clear. The feelings I've been describing are just that: feelings. I don't want to downplay the role or the value of feelings—they're real, and they matter—but sometimes, if we're not careful, they can get out of control and give us a distorted picture of the truth. And these feelings in particular are not grounded in reality. The truth is the Word of God doesn't say that being single is wrong, sinful, or bad.

On the contrary, we know that Paul was all in favor of it:

> Now concerning virgins: I have no commandment from the Lord; yet I give judgment as one whom the Lord in His mercy has made trustworthy. I suppose therefore that this is good because of the present distress—that it is good for a man to remain as he is: Are you bound to a wife? Do not seek to be loosed. Are you loosed from a wife? Do not seek a wife. But even if you do marry, you have not sinned; and if a virgin marries, she has not sinned. Nevertheless such will have trouble in the flesh, but I would spare you. . . .
>
> But I want you to be without care. He who is unmarried cares for the things of the Lord—how he may please the Lord. But he who is married cares about the things of the world—how he may please his wife. There is a difference between a wife and a virgin. The unmarried woman cares about the things of the Lord, that she may be holy both in body and in spirit. But she who is married cares about the things of the world—how she may please her husband. And this I say for your own profit, not that I may put a leash on you, but for what is proper, and that you may serve the Lord without distraction. (1 Cor. 7:25–28, 32–35)

We've all read those verses. They remind us, or should remind us, that singleness is not a moral failing or a cause for shame. On the contrary, the single person has equal worth and dignity with the married person before God.

This should be reason enough for the church to offer the single person genuine acceptance and support. But ask single people if this has been happening in recent years, and you're likely to hear otherwise. Here's what a few of them told me:

> *I sometimes feel isolated, scrutinized, and ignored because the church is by nature a family-oriented community.*—Jim

> *We kind of get shuffled to the background, particularly as adults, because the church doesn't know where to put us within their small group system.*—Charity

> *I wish there was greater understanding that we are not "strange," and [more] intermingling by families with the singles.*—Bea

The evangelical church in general seems to have developed a tendency to rush past those particular verses that elevate singleness, or gloss over them, or explain them away. I've even heard some say that if singles are going to cite Paul's example and advice on singleness, they'd better be prepared to go suffer and give their lives for Christ, as Paul did. For example, here's former Mars Hill Church pastor Mark Driscoll in a sermon on singleness:

> Let's say for example there is a closed Muslim country that desperately needs Jesus. Should I go, with my wife and five kids, or should I have a single guy go and lean over the plate and take one for the team? I should send the single guy, right, because if he's there, and they capture and kill him—which is what they do if you preach the gospel in a Muslim country—at least he doesn't leave behind a widow and orphans.[2]

Thanks, I think.

24

As I wrote earlier, and as some of my interviewees have said, marriage and families have been elevated to such a high status in the church that single people don't always seem to fit anymore or, at worst, seem to have less value than married people—even when we're not being portrayed as cannon fodder! And then when the tough questions I mentioned come up in our minds, the ones that can keep us awake late into the night—*Where did I go wrong? What should I have done differently? Has God forgotten me?*—it's sometimes hard to feel as if we can turn to the church for answers and for help.

I don't say any of this to complain or whine. I want to make the church aware of the experiences of a significant number of its people in the interest of helping the body of Christ learn to recognize and cherish *all* of its members, not just those who happen to fit the ideal of parents/kids/pets. The first step toward changing the church's view of single Christians is to understand what, exactly, that view is and the thinking behind it. This is something I touched on in the introduction to this book. This section will explore it in more detail.

ONE

◆ ◆ ◆

SINGLES AS PROBLEMS

"I'm going to speak of the sin I think besets this generation. It is the sin of delaying marriage as a lifestyle option among those who intend someday to get married, but they just haven't yet. This is a problem shared by men and women, but it's a problem primarily of men."[1]

With those words, spoken at a conference for Christian singles in 2004—and later broadcast on the radio by Dennis Rainey and Bob Lepine of FamilyLife Today—Dr. Al Mohler, then president of the Southern Baptist Theological Seminary, sparked an outcry. Many single Christians wrote to him in protest. *Christianity Today* writer Camerin Courtney, herself a single woman, challenged Mohler's views in a column titled "Is Singleness a Sin?"

"If the reasons for delaying marriage truly are selfishness, childishness, and a purposeful denying of God's will, as Mohler, Rainey, and Lepine assert," Courtney wrote, "then *those* things are the sins—not the resulting singleness. And throwing around the s-word like that, especially toward a group of individuals who already sometimes feel devalued by the church, our families, and sometimes even ourselves, seems not only unscriptural but also irresponsible."[2]

Dr. Mohler eventually clarified:

I stand unmoved, even more convinced that the argument I made at the New Attitude Conference is precisely correct. Singleness is not a sin, but deliberate singleness on the part of those who know they have not been given the gift of celibacy is, at best, a neglect of a Christian responsibility. The problem may be simple sloth, personal immaturity, a fear of commitment, or an unbalanced priority given to work and profession. On the part of men, it may also take the shape of a refusal to grow up and take the lead in courtship. There are countless Christian women who are prayerfully waiting for Christian men to grow up and take the lead. What are these guys waiting for?[3]

In section 2 of this book, we'll take a closer look at some of the ideas about men and women implicit in this passage and how they relate to the current state of affairs among single Christians. But Mohler's statement, as Camerin Courtney suggested, was a sign of a much broader phenomenon within the church. It's the viewing of single people as a problem that needs to be solved.

Note that when Courtney unpacked Mohler's statement, she made a list of qualities that seem to be bound up with singleness, according to his way of looking at the issue: "selfishness, childishness, and a purposeful denying of God's will." She wasn't just extrapolating too much from his words. These are qualities that the church—consciously or unconsciously—often does attribute to single people.

We're often seen as solitary, self-contained, self-sufficient units, blissfully living our own lives without a thought for others.

Naturally, therefore, the increase of singleness within the church is seen as cause for alarm. Look at something else that Mohler said in his original speech: "What is the ultimate priority God has called us to? In heaven, is the crucible of our saint-making going to have been through our jobs? I don't think so. The Scripture makes clear that it will be done largely through our marriages." He also spoke of marriage as "the central crucible for adult-making."[4]

It's not just Mohler, either. Consider for a moment all the messages you've heard through the years from Christian churches and ministries about the importance and value of family. Most likely, they went something like this:

"Motherhood is the most important job in the world."

"Your only real and lasting legacy is your family."

"No one ever said on his deathbed, 'I wish I'd spent more time at work.'"

"If you don't have children, no one will take care of you when you're old/remember you when you're gone."

We're taught, too, that experiencing a faithful marriage and a healthy family life is the best way for Christians to reclaim the culture for God. Here's Candice Watters in her book *Get Married*:

> I was sitting in class [in a graduate program in public policy] learning about all the ways our country was slipping from its constitutional foundation. And in a moment of exasperation, I raised my hand and called out, "So what's the solution?" I

really wanted to know, though I'm not sure I believed there was one. . . .

Dr. Hubert Morken didn't disappoint. He looked at me with a twinkle in his eye and let his grenade fly: "Get married, have babies, and do government! *That's* how we win."[5]

If family life is the highest form of life on earth that Christians can aspire to, and if the family is the exclusive breeding ground of faith and virtue—if, in fact, it's the family that will arrest the decline of Western civilization—then, of course, increasing singleness is going to be a problem. If all this is true, we have around us an increasing number of stunted adults and half-formed saints, unable to reach full maturity or holiness because they're not married.

This view is given even greater credibility by those worrisome statistics I referred to earlier: the ones about cohabitation and extramarital pregnancy rates and other indicators of immorality spiraling out of control. As this one particular aspect of the wider culture—higher rates of singleness—spills into the church, the thinking goes, it must be bringing all those other unsavory trends with it. So it's our duty to urge the singles to marry as soon as possible . . . and if the singles don't or won't or can't get married, that makes them an even bigger problem than they already were.

Eric Reed of *Leadership Journal* frames the issue this way:

Today's young adults are marrying later, if at all, are technologically savvy, and hold worldviews alien to their upbringing. Barna Research president David Kinnaman, after a five-year study, declared that church leaders are unequipped to deal with this "new normal."

. . . Many ignore the situation, hoping young adults' views will be righted when they are older and have their own children. These leaders miss the significance of the shifts of the past 25 years, Kinnaman contends, and the needs for ministry young people have in their present phase—if it is a phase.[6]

Debbie Maken is one author who believes that any attempt to encourage singles to make peace with their state in life is to encourage something unholy. She put it this way in her book *Getting Serious about Getting Married*:

> Being a single person for too long has more capacity to produce negative characteristics in terms of sanctification than it does to produce healthy members of the body of Christ. And yet we persist in our churches to praise the single status, placing it on an equal level with marriage. We delude ourselves and the singles in our congregations into believing that participation in a few service activities will somehow redeem or offset all of the negative practical—and sometimes spiritual—consequences of remaining single despite God's clear call to marriage.[7]

Probably very few Christians in the pews have thought through the issue to this extent, but these teachings—teachings that tell us singleness is a negative condition that needs to be redeemed or offset—do tend to spread throughout the church, often in subtle ways, and they do have an effect. I think they're often behind the ways that people react to our presence in the church—like the woman I met in the ladies' room that time, for instance, or the woman who was struck dumb by my friend Fiona's announcement of her singleness and childlessness . . . or, on a larger scale, the pastors who accuse us of disobeying God's will, or the leaders who shuttle us off to "young adult" ministries when we're well into our thirties and forties. (Frankly, I can't imagine where Maken got the idea that churches have a tendency to "praise the single status." I'm pretty sure the vast majority of single churchgoers will tell you that this has not been their experience at all.)

In a nutshell, if Christians really believe all, or even some, of this to be true—even at a subconscious level—then it's going to affect how they feel about the singles in their midst . . . not to mention how the singles feel about themselves and each other. It's true that, for many of us, there are times when we consider our singleness and all that goes with it a problem. But leaving that question aside for the moment, it's indisputable that to consider *people* a problem is something quite different—and damaging.

TWO

◆ ◆ ◆

SINGLES AS PARIAHS

[If asked what I'd like to say to my church about these issues,] I'd praise their efforts in preaching God's Word but let them know that there is a lot of subliminal messaging saying being single is less desirable than being married with children.—Robyn

Being told, "Maybe you have the gift of singleness" [when someone] desperately wants to get married isn't going to comfort that person; it is going to make them feel even more inadequate, because it is a reminder of their failure—either to find a spouse or to accept being single with happiness. I believe a true gift of singleness is the ability to be completely content in your singleness. It is not adapting to singleness out of despair or because you have no alternative.—Charity

Message directed at women [by the church]: women are not fully adult, fully human, or fully complete if

they are not married. Marriage is a reward, and if you aren't married, then maybe it's because there are areas of sin or spiritual growth that need to be addressed in order to make you "ready." Message directed at both [men and women]: singles groups are the "holding pen" between youth/college and full adulthood where you are to mix and mingle only with other singles in order to find your mate and "graduate" to big church.—Fiona

Many of the teachings and aphorisms I've referred to, about the great value of marriage and family, contain some truth. They're meant to remind us of just how crucial family relationships are to each one of us and to society in general, and in that they usually succeed.

But I would argue that if we elevate marriage and family so high that we begin to act as if they're the most important elements of Christianity—even more important than our salvation through Christ—we have a real problem, and it's *not* the number of singles. Getting our priorities out of whack like this is downright dangerous. It encourages us to place our greatest faith and hope in something other than God, and instead of drawing people to Christ it drives them away.

The next time you hear a Christian equate marriage with godliness, or say something about marriage and children being the best things in life, or express the thought that "You're not complete unless you're married," as Maureen, one of my interviewees, remembers hearing—the kind of thing that is said so casually and so frequently—stop a minute and consider these ideas from the perspective of a person who's single and childless, and not necessarily by choice.

Imagine how brutally they might fall on your ear if you had no spouse and no children.

In her book *Cupid Is a Procrastinator: Making Sense of the Unexpected Single Life*, Kate Hurley recalls the time she had to ask a friend and mentor to stop implying that her singleness was her own fault for not following all the correct formulas (just "let go" and sit there and wait for God to bring your husband):

> I finally say, "Em, please understand me here. If you had a friend who was having multiple miscarriages or had been struggling with barrenness for ten years, would you say to her 'Well, if you just trusted the Lord more with your barrenness, he would give you a baby'? You would never say that! You would recognize how much she mourns the loss, and you would be sensitive in your words. You wouldn't want to hurt her by saying her struggle was her own fault. At times I feel barren—not only barren as a mother, but barren as a lover, as well. Please, please be sensitive to this barrenness in me. Please don't tell me that I have done something wrong and that the result of my shortcoming is barrenness."[1]

Hurley acknowledges that many times these formulas are offered to us by married people who actually want to help and just don't know how else to do it. But that doesn't make them any easier or less painful for us to hear. The fact that these things are so easily believed and so frequently said to singles, and that singles have to push back against them to avoid being misunderstood and judged, shows the church abdicating an important duty.

Sketchy theology has other consequences as well. It can lead, for instance, to particularly harsh treatment for those singles with a divorce in their past, so harsh that, as Jeremy

Myers wrote, they're made to feel that they've committed "the unforgivable sin."[2] My interviewee Jim told me something about the confusing and discouraging things divorced persons tend to hear in church:

> *Honestly, the messages from elders and pastors on re-marriage are mixed. I have been told it would be a sin to marry another, even though the marriage ended because of the reasons cited in Scripture. I've heard from others that being born again is a new life altogether and it is allowable to remarry.*

Sketchy theology can also lead to double standards. My interviewee Carole recalls an experience that many single women go through:

> *In my early forties I was really struggling with not ever having a baby. There was a woman in my church— a married woman who was not able to conceive. She would cry and the women would rally. Try doing that when you are single—you get no response. You get told to accept God's will and not to be angry with God. . . . We are not allowed to grieve a loss of children? Or a loss of our dreams and our desires? When we do, we are whining and ungrateful. Of course, no one says that—but their inconsiderate actions do.*

Setting the Solitary in Families

Paul's portrait of the church throughout the New Testament is of something more than a community—it's "one body," tightly knit together, each part functioning not just for itself but for others. In this body, each member needs all the others and, ideally, knows the value of all the others. At its best, the strong are there to support the weak, and the lonely are comforted and encouraged. At its best, the church lives out the truth of Psalm 68:6: "God sets the solitary in families."

But what happens when the church—consciously or unconsciously—elevates married people over single people? Unfortunately, there's a lot of twisted thinking that goes with that, which, as we've seen, can lead to quite a lot of hurtful behavior. Instead of helping to set the solitary in families, the church in such cases can end up making them feel even more solitary.

My church body itself has been influential only at a relational level through mentoring relationships with older women—which have been much more valuable than any "retreats" or "dating talks."—Ashley

Many singles are hungry for the kind of mentoring relationships, or even just friendships, with more mature Christians that Ashley describes. In her book *The Dating Manifesto*, Lisa Anderson writes of signing up for her church's mentoring program and being assigned to an older married woman, Kathy. At their first meeting, Kathy said to Lisa and her friends, "You should know up front that you women terrify me."

Anderson continues:

We found out in talking with her that she felt pretty uncomfortable with the idea of mentoring single girls. She married young and her assumptions about us were that we lived exciting, fast-paced lives with amazing careers and varied experiences. She wondered what she had to offer us. After all, she had "only" been a stay-at-home mom. She knew diapers, carpools, and football practice. She feared that was all she knew.

But we had to tell her that *she* was where we wanted to be. . . . It took a lot of convincing on our part to get her to accept her story as one that was valuable to us. It also was a big job to show her that *single* isn't synonymous with *alien*.[3]

There are a number of factors at work here. There's a lack of understanding, even a kind of fear, of people who have lived a different kind of life story. There's a tendency to make groundless assumptions. Paradoxically, considering that we've been talking about the widespread view that singleness is wrong and singles are inferior, this woman even felt inferior around singles!

Here's another relevant story, from my interviewee Allison:

In the past year or so I moved . . . and started attending a fairly large church. Due to the size, it's very important to get involved outside of the Sunday service if you want to really connect with your fellow attendees. I decided the best way to do this was to join a "small group," which the church regularly encouraged people to attend. After taking the first "intro" class on how to join a small group, we were informed that we could choose what kind of group we wanted to connect with: married with young children, empty nesters, widows, singles, single again, or mixed life stages. I decided I wanted the chance to connect with people in various life stages (I mean, I know what older single twentysomethings struggle with, so why do I need more of that perspective?), so I marked that on the form. The next week started week one of three weeks of classes to establish these groups. When I arrived, the gentleman at the door quickly informed me that the singles table was in the back. I happily said, "Actually I was hoping to join the mixed life stages group." He looked at me for a few seconds and said, "Well, see the mixed life stages tables over there? They are mostly in their fifties and those tables are already really full." I decided to brave the fifty-year-olds anyway and joined their table. They all looked very surprised to see me sit there, and one couple even remarked that they had daughters my age at the singles table. . . . I shared that I felt I knew what individuals my age were dealing with and was looking for other perspectives. I also wanted to learn from others and perhaps be able to share with them things that I had learned. In the end it's been a wonderful experience, but from my church's small group pastor's teachings in the class, his thoughts on community would [involve] separating into little pockets of those in the exact same life stages.

Imagine just how many Kathys and Allisons might be out there, feeling separated from women with different marital statuses by these artificial and needless barriers. The teachings we've been looking at, and a magnification of the differences between us (real differences, yes, but not always as important as we make them out to be), can lead to a mixture of condemnation and envy.

Be honest: If you're a churchgoer who's married with children, have you ever looked at that single and childless man or woman in your pew and had a thought like this strike you?

"She doesn't know how good she has it."

"I wish *I* only had to think about myself."

"I wish I could sleep in every morning like him."

"It would be so nice to be free like him, to do whatever I wanted."

"She thinks she's tired just because she has a hard job? She doesn't know the meaning of the word *tired*!"

And the one I hate the most: "Well, until she has kids, she'll never know real love/understand what life is really about."

Perhaps you personally have never indulged in such reflections. But we know that some married Christians really are thinking these things. We know because some people actually slip now and then and say them out loud. We know we're often seen as the Peter Pans of the church, the flighty ones who refuse to grow up.

More than that, we're often portrayed as everything that's wrong with the modern world. If that sounds like an exaggeration, stop and think for a minute about what you've read, seen, or heard about single people lately. Maybe a couple of those memes popped up in your Facebook feed—the ones about how single women are too independent or aren't into cooking or cleaning like they should be, and so it's no wonder they can't get a man. Maybe you saw one of those articles listing all the ways that selfish, hedonistic singles are destroying the country (usually with accompanying photo of Lena Dunham from HBO's sexually explicit *Girls* as a visual aid).

Maybe, without realizing it, you started to internalize all of this and let it color your view of single people.

Here's what you need to know: every time you've shared one of those memes, every time you've hit "like" on one of those articles, every time you've enthusiastically contributed to one of those Facebook threads about the wantonness of single women or the patheticness of single men, the single people in your church were watching. And they were internalizing something too. They were internalizing your low view of their value and worth.

"But that's not what I meant!" you may be saying to yourself right now. "I was just thinking of *a certain type* of single person." It probably never occurred to you to associate the villainous, civilization-destroying stereotype in those memes with that nice young single man or woman who works on food drives or helps teach a Sunday school class or sings in the choir.

If that's your mindset, or if you even have reason to suspect that it might be, here are a couple of questions to ask yourself:

1. Even if you really are able to keep all those different kinds of singles successfully compartmentalized in your head, is demonizing one particular kind of single—any kind—really the loving Christian thing to do? Is it the kind of action that will draw people to a loving and forgiving Christ?

2. Even if you are keeping them compartmentalized, are you sure that nice young single person at church is able to do so? Are you sure that he or she isn't hearing your words, watching your online activity, and thinking that you're just bashing single people in general?

If you happen to be a parent, here's something else to consider. You probably expect that all your kids will be married one day. Most likely they will. But, as I hope I've managed to make clear by now, there are no guarantees.

So imagine your young son or daughter many years from now as a single adult, with his or her sense of self-worth suffering the death of a thousand cuts at the hands of fellow Christians. For as hard as we try, many of us can't help letting those perceptions and those judgments shape our lives more than we should.

Embracing Life

On some level, we're aware that our lives would be more honoring to God and more fulfilling for ourselves if we were to embrace our stage in life and learn to live life to the fullest. At the same time, we're acutely aware of how our fellow Christians tend to see us and we're sometimes afraid to be seen embracing our lives *too* much, lest we confirm the worst stereotypes about ourselves—the stereotypes we carry in our own minds as well as those imposed on us from outside.

But this would be living a lie, and as Christians that is the last thing we're supposed to do. I appreciate the fact that Lydia Brownback wrote a whole book about the idea that we're allowed to live full lives when we're single, called *Fine China Is for Single Women Too*. Here's the anecdote that inspired the title:

> Single women put a lot of things on hold because they are afraid that investing in or committing to or being associated with them might keep them locked in the single life. After attending five bridal showers over the course of a year, a single friend of mine had begun to envy the beautiful place settings, the Waterford goblets, and the flatware. She finally realized, "Who says marriage and good dishes must go together?" My friend entertains frequently and loves to cook.

So she went shopping and selected a china pattern that she admired. She began collecting one plate at a time. Her family also enjoyed adding to her collection at Christmas and on her birthday. She now has place settings for eight, and the exercise of hospitality is much easier.

When the obstacle isn't financial, why don't more domestically minded single women do the same thing? It is because they are waiting for the bridal shower. Somehow they imagine that venturing forth solo into domesticity as maneuvering into sacred marital territory, a mindset that leaves them feeling left out of the good life. These women also hold back for fear that venturing out will more firmly entrench them in singleness.[4]

Another story along these lines that I love comes from one of my favorite actors, Sir Alec Guinness. This isn't a story of singleness, but it is one about refusing to let unwanted circumstances dictate our choices and our lives—a topic with which most single people are very familiar.

Guinness was born to an unwed mother and grew up in poverty, not knowing who his father was. But he hoped to find out when he turned twenty-one and perhaps receive a message or even a gift from his father. After his birthday, he went to see the family lawyer, who claimed to know nothing at all about his parentage.

> Shyly, and in a small voice, I asked, "Is there anything for me? I mean, I was told when I was twenty-one there would be something coming to me."
> "Such as?"
> "I'm not sure. A gold watch, perhaps."
> "A gold watch? Never heard of it. Some delusion of your mother's I'd guess. I am sorry, but there is nothing."[5]

Guinness never did find out for certain who his father was. But many years later, he wrote,

> With my first week's salary from [T. S.] Eliot's *The Cocktail Party* I bought myself the gold vest-pocket watch that had never materialised and always wore it during the play. On the inside I had engraved, "The readiness is all" [from *Hamlet*]. Not that I have ever felt really ready for anything; but in an obscure way I suppose I felt I had arrived—somewhere, somehow, and from God knows where.[6]

What I love about this story is Guinness's refusal to let his fatherlessness define or destroy him. This is so unlike the narratives we sometimes hear from the modern church, the ones in which fatherlessness dooms you, or at the very least places you in a position where all kinds of bad things are destined to keep happening to you and good things are destined to steer clear of you. Instead, when life refused to hand out prizes to him, like a traditional twenty-first birthday gift from a father to a son, Guinness awarded himself his own prize, meaningful in its own way because he earned it through hard work.

This is the kind of story that can inspire a single person to overcome the bitterness of not receiving the expected from life and to set out to create new dreams, goals, and expectations. It shows us that, even when we have to do without some of the greatest blessings in life, like a parent or a spouse, hardship does not have to have the final say over the way we live our lives.

So it truly is important for single people to enjoy, even treasure, certain freedoms. Singleness has its benefits and blessings, as do most stages in life. As Lisa Anderson writes,

"I don't think these perks are overrated. They're not consolation prizes for missing out on anniversary dinners and the pitter-patter of little feet. I don't think they should be downplayed or apologized for, either."[7]

I concur. As a single person, I've had opportunities—educational opportunities, opportunities to travel, and more—that I might never have had if I were married with children. I've thoroughly enjoyed these blessings and am deeply grateful to God for them.

The trouble comes when blessings like these make us the subject of envy and resentment—especially since, for most of us, they're something we didn't exactly ask for. When you ask God for one good thing (marriage) and get a different good thing instead, you can enjoy and celebrate what you were given, but that doesn't mean you don't mourn what you've lost.

Sometimes, hearing that it's okay to cry just because being single is hard does me a world of good.—Chrissy

And when others see only the good side of your singleness and refuse you the right to lament the bad side, that only makes the wound deeper. When you can't say you're tired without someone retorting that you don't have a family so you don't know the first thing about tiredness, it tends to shut down conversation, put up walls, and make you feel very lonely and misunderstood. After a while, you start feeling like you have to justify and qualify every word that comes out of your mouth: "I'm really tired today—but I know I'm not *nearly* as tired as you! I couldn't ever possibly be as tired as you!"

Let me stress that I'm not for a minute denying the truth of that statement. I may come home from work exhausted, but I'm not as exhausted as the mom who comes home from work and has to feed the kids dinner and supervise homework and wash muddy soccer uniforms and make school lunches and do a hundred other child-related tasks. Fair enough. But do we always have to turn everything into a game of "Can you top this?" Can we not learn to reach across the barriers and commiserate with each other a little, instead of constantly trying to portray each other's experiences as less valid than our own?

Besides, let's not forget that you married people have a leg up on us when it comes to division of labor! Next time your spouse is mowing the lawn while you make lunch, or taking your car to get the oil changed and the tires rotated while you do the taxes, or vacuuming while you do the laundry, or chipping the ice off your windshield while you get to stay in the warm house a few minutes longer, think about the single person in your church or your neighborhood who, unless he or she has kind friends or relatives nearby, gets to do all of it without help.

> I have never married and have no kids, yet women much younger than me with older kids get all kinds of help if their husbands are sick or die. What about us—are we valuable? . . . Single women especially face some issues of security and needs for help, and I always have to ask. Most of the time I pay people to help me when married or widowed women would be offered help for free. . . . It's not what churches do that is so upsetting—it is what they don't do.—Carole

In addition to this, the contributions we make to the church are not always noticed; in fact, we're often told that we should be doing more. And even when we spend lavishly on wedding gifts and baby showers for our fellow church members, people don't always think to do something nice for us on special occasions in our lives, such as a birthday, a move, or a promotion. As Christians, of course, we're supposed to learn to do good without hope of being noticed or rewarded for it in this life—but in the context of church life, it sometimes seems that singles are given many more opportunities to learn it than married people are!

There are exceptions to this: for instance, a single woman at my former church who earned her PhD was congratulated and celebrated by fellow churchgoers for her accomplishment. I was moved and impressed by that. It would be really nice to see more of that kind of thing happening, because too often we "selfish singles" end up contributing to everyone else's celebrations with no hope of any kind of reciprocation. Not that we do it for reciprocation, but let me be honest: there are moments when it's just painful to know there may never be any.

My interviewee Lynn belongs to a church where all members, married and single, are required to serve in the nursery on a rotating basis. She told me:

Yes, I feel that parents need a break from their children and they can benefit from attending church without worrying about their children. Where is the balance in serving, though? Where is the give and take? If I'm helping in the nursery, I think it would be appropriate to [have] a married couple reciprocate by having the husband help me with a household fix-it job that I don't know how to do or have the right tools to do. . . . The church is looking out for the married couples' needs but not the singles' needs in a lot of cases. While I don't think the church actually sees us as second best, that is the message that is coming across. I also think that sort of arrangement (singles serving in the nursery, and couples helping singles in other ways) would foster an awesome sense of community.

Again, I'm not downplaying the tremendous responsibilities and difficulties of marriage and parenthood or minimizing families' need for the church's help and support. I've been helping care for kids since I got my first babysitting job at age eleven; I know a bit about how strenuous it is. I know about the vomit and the fighting and the blowout diapers and the midnight screaming and the endless questions . . . and I've never had to handle it 24/7, year in and year out! I can only begin to imagine what you parents go through, and believe me, my hat is off to you.

All I'm saying is the various members of the church may have different sorts of burdens to bear, some heavier than others, but we should still be willing to listen and support each other instead of always trying to one-up each other. When Paul wrote, "Bear one another's burdens, and so fulfill the law of Christ" (Gal. 6:2), he did not add, "But first weigh them carefully to make sure the other person's burden is the same weight as yours." He was interested only in our sharing them with each other and helping to lighten them for each other.

Do you want to know the biggest irony in all this? While some church members are looking down on singles for their perceived selfishness or even their perceived disobedience, quite a few single Christians are practicing obedience to God at a level that many of those who married young may never reach.

Living Sacrifices

> I beseech you therefore, brethren, by the mercies of God, that you present your bodies a living sacrifice, holy, acceptable to God, which is your reasonable service. (Rom. 12:1)

For single people in the church, Romans 12:1 has special and significant implications. It carries with it a requirement that's harder than ever to meet in this day and age, when it often seems that the entire world is pitted against our efforts to meet it. Many of us are in the position that the demon Screwtape describes in C. S. Lewis's *The Screwtape Letters*:

> Our cause is never more in danger than when a human, no longer desiring, but still intending, to do our Enemy's will, looks round upon a universe from which every trace of Him seems to have vanished, and asks why he has been forsaken, and still obeys.[8]

I can relate to the person in that example more and more as the years go by. For instance, in my younger days, when I was dealing with the monthly pain and mess and inconvenience of what my family euphemistically calls "the curse," I used to say to my mother, "I'd *better* have a baby to make all this worth it!" I said it jokingly, never doubting in those days that it would actually happen.

I don't say that anymore. These days, every "curse" reminds me of what it's increasingly likely I'll never have. Just like every Facebook photo of a happy family with their newborn. Just like every baby shower invitation. I'm sincerely happy for those so blessed, but there's pain on these occasions too. It's nobody's fault, certainly not that of the happy families. I want to rejoice with those who rejoice; I do my best to rejoice with them, and I believe it's good and healthy, even godly, for me to do so. But it costs me something, all the same.

And the church's attitude toward the unmarried and childless can make it hurt all the more. Imagine being blamed because you don't have something that you want very badly. Now take it a step further and imagine that one reason you don't have what you want is that you've carefully followed the teachings of the people who are now blaming you.

As Amanda McCracken writes in an article titled "When True Love Keeps Waiting":

> What happens when women and men who have kept their promise to save their virginity for that person are 30-plus and still unmarried?
>
> I want to believe that God rewards the faithful like the old mother Elizabeth, the forgiving brother Joseph, the widowed peasant Ruth, and the all-enduring Job, but it feels like I've waited so long. Imagine a child told if she had perfect attendance for the school year, she'd be rewarded in the end—but the school year keeps going long enough that even the administrators wonder why she still refuses to miss school.[9]

McCracken was speaking, as am I, as a Christian who believes that sexual activity belongs exclusively within marriage —which means, I'm afraid, that we're speaking as members of a minority. Consider a few statistics:

A recent study reveals that 88 percent of unmarried young adults (ages 18–29) are having sex. The same study, conducted by The National Campaign to Prevent Teen and Unplanned Pregnancy, reveals the number doesn't drop much among Christians. Of those surveyed who self-identify as "evangelical," 80 percent say they have had sex.[10]

Consider also the anecdotal evidence I can tell you from my own experience, and that many other single Christians could tell you from theirs. Like the large numbers of people on dating sites who call themselves "Christian" but are all in favor of premarital sex. Or the nominally Christian man on one dating site who scolded me for putting in my profile that pornography use by a man was a deal-breaker for me. (Or all the other Christian men who scolded me for not being nice or understanding enough about the issue when I wrote publicly about that scolding.[11])

One particular dating site has many specific questions people can answer about their opinions and preferences, including a question about at which point in a relationship they prefer to begin having sex. This is how I know that the site is full of men who identify as Christian and would like to start having sex within the first six dates. And women too, I'm sure, though I'm not set up to be able to see other female profiles. It's possible that some of them are exaggerating or lying to make themselves appear more interesting and attractive, but even so, what does that say about their values?

Let me make one thing clear. I'm not here to judge or shame my fellow Christians. We're all sinners, myself not least, which means that we've all gone against the faith we profess at various times and in various ways. To put it more simply, we all make mistakes.

What I find remarkable is the attitude that determines beforehand that mistakes are either (1) acceptable or (2) not mistakes at all. Or even, for many, (3) absolute requirements. It's one thing to sin, but when one fully intends to sin and makes it clear from the outset that sin is a must in a dating relationship, I feel like we're playing a whole different ball game.

That paradigm—the attitude that "if you want to date me, of course we're going to have sex, Christian beliefs notwithstanding"—has led many Christians to compromise their standards, and it's left others feeling lonely, bruised, and forsaken. It is not an easy thing to back out of a promising relationship, or even refrain from starting a relationship, because one realizes that it's heading inexorably in a direction dishonoring to God. Without the loving support of friends, family, or a church community, too many have found themselves giving in.

My interviewee Erin actually told me:

It has been my experience as an older single person that the Christian men I date are mostly interested in talking about sex and often press me to have sex outside of marriage. I have not found the same thing with the men I date who are not believers.

Of course, anyone can call himself or herself a Christian on a dating site. If it were easier to meet someone at church, it would be easier to find someone who shared similar ideas and values and to get an idea of whether that person was a nominal or a sincere Christian. And maybe we'd be spared some of those awkward conversations about our sex lives, or lack thereof, with prospective partners whom we've just met. Trust me, I could very happily go the rest of my life without having to write to a stranger, "Could you please clarify what you meant when you included 'sexually knowledgeable' in your must-haves?" ever again.

It's not just an online problem, either. Anywhere we go that we're likely to meet potential dates—parties or dances or classes or Meetup groups or anywhere else you can think of—we have to take into account that most, maybe all, of those potential dates have a completely different set of values. Crazy as it sounds, those of us who are determined to date in accordance with our Christian conscience often find ourselves in situations where we have to be ready to attract and repel simultaneously. And sometimes, when you're longing to meet someone, the repelling part is really, really hard.

Which would seem to make church a welcome alternative. But it's not that easy to meet someone at church—not anymore. A study done in 2009 on "How straight couples met their partners" showed that "in church" was the *least* popular answer. More couples had met through friends, at a bar or restaurant, online, through coworkers, in college, through family, through neighbors, or through school than through church.[12]

> *It's quite difficult to meet other young single Christians. There really aren't many functions that have the purpose of meeting other single Christians with the possibility of dating. There are many where that is a byproduct. I don't know of a better way to solve this; it's just difficult when Christ is the most important thing in a relationship and yet there don't seem [to be] many ways to meet other like-minded people looking for a relationship within the church.*—Scott

In our parents' and grandparents' world, so we're told, high standards would help you find a spouse worth having; in our world, high standards are likely to have you sitting home alone watching TV on Saturday night. Thank God, there are still those Christians who find fellow Christians with similar values and are able to get married. But the plain truth is many other Christians have had to compromise their principles in order to find someone to marry.

And yet Christian leaders as a group are inclined to hold up the married as our examples to follow, regardless of how they achieved that status, while treating the singles as problem children. We've been taught that one is rewarded in this world for doing right when our teachers should have known—from the past two millennia of Christian history, if from nothing else—that very often the reward will not come in this lifetime. That, in fact, what we receive in this lifetime may actually look more like punishment.

Anthony Esolen put it beautifully in *First Things*:

Let me speak up for the young people who do in fact follow the moral law and the teachings of the Church. Many of these are suffering intense loneliness. Have you bothered to notice? Have you considered all those young people who want to be married, who should be married, but who, because they will not play evil's game, can find no one to marry? The girls who at age twenty-five and older have never even been asked on a date? The "men" languishing in a drawn-out adolescence? These people are among us; they are everywhere. Who gives them a passing thought? They are suffering for their faith, and no one cares. Do you care, leaders of my Church? . . .

What help do you give them? Do you not rather at every step exacerbate their suffering, when by your silence and your telling deeds you confirm in them the terrible fear *that they have been played for chumps, that their own leaders do not believe, that they would have been happier in this world had they gone along with the world, and that their leaders would have smiled upon them had they done so?*[13]

If you're a celibate Christian who's ever known that sinking feeling in your gut when you pursued a promising match online only to find that the person was looking for a "sexually knowledgeable" partner, you know exactly what he's talking about. In fact, when the church gives this impression, it contributes to the problem of single Christians giving in to sexual temptation, or even making premarital sexual activity a "must-have." As Amanda McCracken writes, "Plenty of women come to this decision as a way to try to fix dysfunctional relationships, or to address our own hangups over fear, shame, or low self-esteem."[14] Too often, no one in the church has been there to help them with those emotions; instead, they've been reinforcing the shame and the low self-esteem.

When one of my married friends found out I was writing this book, she was eager to talk to me about her own experiences in her single days. I found her story fascinating, as she came relatively late to the sexualized culture we know so well and was able to bring an outsider's perspective to it. She had had a strict Catholic upbringing in Europe and sincerely believed that she would go to hell if she had sex before marriage. But she moved to America at eighteen and was shell-shocked to find a completely different milieu from the one in which she had grown up. Suddenly she felt like the only virgin around, she said, and "Everyone was telling me how weird I was."

She held out for a number of years, but it grew more and more difficult as she felt utterly without support. It was hard to find a man who was patient with her stance, and even her mother started to think she was weird for waiting. "I didn't know where to turn," she told me, and in the end she gave in and slept with her boyfriend just to feel like a normal person. All these years later, she still regrets that she didn't hold to her convictions.

My friend's church had taught her spiritual and moral lessons but had never tried to prepare her for a culture in which premarital sex was completely normalized. And it had not given her the kind of support she needed to face such a culture. Without these things, even the staunchest convictions can be terribly hard to hold on to.

In a way, as someone who left one culture in her home country for a very different culture here in America, my friend was in an unusual position. In another way, it wasn't unusual at all, for a Christian. All of us who attend church regularly—single and married alike—live in two different cultures, and sometimes we can't shuttle back and forth between the two without feeling a fair amount of culture shock. All of us walk out into a world full of temptations, moral conflicts, and compromises when the sermon or the Sunday school class is finished. And all of us need help taking what we've learned in one place and applying it to the other.

Single Christians practicing celibacy are no exception to that. In fact, in some ways, we're an extreme example. The world often simply cannot comprehend why we choose to live as we do. If we're already committed to someone, that's one thing; but a healthy, red-blooded single American adult choosing not to have sex when the opportunity arises simply because of some archaic religious belief? Lunacy!

So if you've never been in the sort of situation that Esolen describes or that my friend described, count your blessings—and try to be aware that these things are going on all around you, in the lives of an increasing number of your fellow churchgoers. And ask yourself how—even in the midst of a busy life—you can show a little kindness, compassion, and sympathy. We need your support more than you can know.

THREE

◆ ◆ ◆

SINGLES AS PROJECTS

[Some say] that singles should just get married . . . like, what are we waiting for, that it is our own doing. . . . I desire to be married. I definitely don't desire to be single for the rest of my life, but I don't feel like I'm unreasonably "picky" or at fault for not being married yet.—Lynn

It is generally assumed that the goal of all singles is to find a mate and that the primary purpose singles are in the church is to find a mate, so they are lumped together as often as possible and teaching is directed at becoming the sort of person you need to be in order to get a mate.—Fiona

Sometimes what I hear [from the church] is that men need to step up and act like men. Actually, a lot of the time I hear that—Mark Driscoll preaches here in Seattle,[1] and he has a very pro-manliness take on all

this. However, he also will make remarks about women not being attractive enough or "letting themselves go," which is troubling.—Michelle

When we speak of "help," as Esolen does, we need to be very clear about what we're saying. There's a kind of help that really helps, and then there's a kind that does more harm than good. The latter kind can make us feel more ostracized and more inferior than ever.

I believe God has a plan for my life, but I often struggle to reconcile that belief with my own disappointment and the pressure I've experienced from other Christians. I believe in my head that if I'm still single at this point, having tried to follow God's leading for my life, then He must have good reasons for that. But too often, I believe in my heart that I must have messed up somehow. *If I just had tried harder, dated more, been sweeter or prettier, worn more makeup, worn less makeup, joined just a few more social groups, gone to just a few more activities, then maybe . . .*

In my more rational moments, I don't believe that's what God would say to me. But it's the kind of thing well-meaning Christians say to single people all the time. If we're problems and pariahs, then it stands to reason that the next step is to make us into projects—malfunctioning objects that need to be fixed.

Not Good Enough

I once wrote an article for *Christianity Today* trying to highlight some of the Christian messages constantly being thrown our way by showing how they affect one hypothetical single girl. Allow me, if you will, to quote myself on the subject. Just an excerpt should give you the gist:

> The girl dated around for a while, but nothing seemed to work out. She remembered her high standards and tried her best to be faithful to them. She wasn't going to settle for a young man who wasn't strong in his faith, mature, well-mannered, and kind.
>
> And the knowing ones shook their heads and said, "You're too picky."
>
> So the girl tried harder to make things work. She tried to give every reasonably decent guy every chance she could. She spent as much time as she could with as many Christian guys as she could.
>
> And the knowing ones shook their heads and said, "You're spending too much time just being friends with guys. They need to know you're romantically interested."
>
> The girl worked on learning to show she was romantically interested. She tried to smile and flirt and be nice and dress prettily. And the knowing ones shook their heads and said, "Watch it, you're being too forward. Let the man pursue you. They don't like it when you do the pursuing."
>
> So the girl worked on being passive. She was quiet and meek and let the guys start every conversation.[2]

And so on, and so on, and so on. That article won third place in the humor category of a Christian journalism competition, which made me feel honored but also a little bemused, because it wasn't meant to be funny. It was meant to be truthful. It is, in fact, the reality that many Christian women and men are living right now.

On his popular blog *Stuff Christians Like*, Jon Acuff once created "The Surviving Church as a Single Scorecard." The idea was that a single got points for every experience listed on the card that he or she had undergone. For example:

> Someone told you, "If you stop looking for love you'll find it." 2 points for each time you've heard that. . . .
>
> Someone you just met for the first time said a sentence like this to you, "If you want to get married, you need to _____." = + 2 points . . .
>
> Someone has quoted the "it's not good for man to be alone" Bible verse to you. = + 2 points . . .
>
> Someone told you, "Maybe you need to focus on being more like a Proverbs 31 woman." = 2 points for each time it wasn't sincere encouragement. . . .
>
> To justify giving a four week marriage sermon series to a congregation that is 60% single, the pastor throws out one blanket statement like this at the beginning of the series, "And you single people listen up to this too, this will serve you well when you get married too." = +2 points.[3]

You get the idea. Single Christians from all over wrote in to report sky-high scores.

I realize that if I put more time and effort in, I could possibly be in a relationship. But I also have a belief that both my time and marriage in general are to be for God. Not to say I relinquish either of those to Him fully, as I should, but those are my goals and I strive to keep those values in the forefront as I struggle with the loneliness of being single. On the other hand, I also believe that if marriage is to be for God, it is a most sacred calling and not to be entered into lightly. In some ways, singleness frees me for other things, and in other ways, it burdens me emotionally. I believe that God has sovereign control, however, and if it were His plan for me to be married, that I would be. On the other hand, I also believe in free will, so I cannot say it is entirely outside of God's will. I suppose I subscribe to the thinking that I should wait for God's best for me. I don't say God's best in the sense that there are men that are not good enough, I only mean God's best in the sense of compatibility and life purpose/interests.—Bea

I think in many ways the church promotes the idea that if you follow the rules [and] honor the Lord with all you have, including your life plan, He will in turn bless you with the desires of your heart, which often means an amazing godly husband. I also think that many churches haven't addressed the changes in our culture regarding individuals getting married later, delayed adolescences, etc.—Allison

We single Christians constantly deal with this inner tension between the good things the church has taught us—God has a plan for our lives and is lovingly guiding us—and the not-so-good things—if we're single, we must have done something wrong and we need to be whipped into shape! The result can be a stiflingly rule-bound view of human relationships. This is how even churches that hold to a grace-filled view of God can end up teaching a legalistic view of humanity. We're told we'll get the attention, the respect, and, yes, the love we desire if we can just make ourselves into better, worthier, more beautiful people.

In her book *Who's Picking Me Up from the Airport? and Other Questions Single Girls Ask*, Cindy Johnson remembers growing up in church with this philosophy ingrained in her:

"If I carefully lived up to my future husband's ideal-wife list—some hybrid of a Proverbs 31 woman and a super sexy model who stayed quiet—God would bring me my soul mate and we'd live happily ever after."[4] As for the guys she met at Christian college, Johnson recalls, "Most of them seemed to think God would deliver a virgin Jessica Alba if they went to church regularly and didn't sleep with their girlfriends. Apparently the guys were sold some bad dating advice along the way too."[5]

The tiny sliver of truth embedded in some of these teachings makes them all the more insidious and powerful. Of course it's important to take care of ourselves and pay attention to the impression we make. Of course a well-groomed, well-mannered person is likelier to catch the interest of the opposite sex. That's just plain common sense. But somewhere along the way, this truth has been twisted into the belief that however well-groomed and well-mannered we are, if we haven't found a mate yet, then it's not enough. We have to keep pushing ourselves. We have to be *more* attractive, *more* fit, *more* personable. Men have to be more willing to step up and take charge; women have to be more willing to sit back, be sweet and quiet and passive, and let them take charge.

And if we can't achieve that perfect combination of qualities that will get us what we want, then we just have to try even harder. Because if this formula doesn't work, if we fail to reach the goal of marriage, then we blew it. It's all our fault.

My Facebook friend Joanna puts it this way:

Contentment takes on strange and mythical powers in the eyes of some Christians. Spouse-attracting powers, to be exact. Many times I've been told that God would send along a boyfriend once I learned to be content with singleness.

Don't hear me wrong; I believe in contentment and hope to achieve it someday. It seems like a very emotionally healthy thing to have. Anyway, it's biblical so I kinda have to be content with the idea of contentment. There just seems to be a bit of a logical flaw in using contentment as a tool to get something you are discontent about. It stretches the definition of contentment a little too far. I'm pretty sure God is not easily fooled by our attempts to fake contentment in order to get something anyway. He would be able to work out what we are trying to do. Such a view also portrays God as a bit of a sadist—refusing to give us what we deeply desire and then springing it on us when we don't really want it anymore. Our lame attempts to fake contentment probably entertain him at least.

There is also a bit of a sinister underside to this problem. It is often not noticed and probably isn't usually intended, but it is there. The subtext of the statement is that marriage is the reward for people who have gotten it together spiritually whereas singleness is the punishment and remedial bootcamp for those who haven't managed yet.[6]

This is how the poison of false teachings about singleness, dating, and marriage can leak into our larger view of the world, of faith, and of God. When you hear that whisper of "You're not good enough to catch a man/attract a woman" too often, it's easy to internalize that as *You're not good enough—period*. Never mind that our faith isn't even supposed to be about being "good enough." Never mind the grace of God that saved us or the work of the Holy Spirit in our lives. Hearing these rules-based messages all the time can catch us in an endless loop of perfectionism that can do serious damage to both our walk with God and our sense of self. If it goes on long enough, we can start to feel that no one could possibly love us as we are—that whether we're worthy of love depends on our ability to perform.

Cindy Johnson spells out the natural result of this thinking:

> Somewhere inside, I started to believe that God worked love out for those worth loving. The fact that it didn't go well for me meant that something was wrong with me. The good people get chosen. The rest of us don't.[7]

I've taken a few steps down this road before—though not to the point where it seriously harmed my faith, I'm thankful to say. In the past, I've made a serious effort to lose a few pounds, grow out my hair to what Candice Watters calls "a more feminine length,"[8] and push myself to try new activities, all in order to win over a man. I'm not saying all this was a total waste of time; the effort may have done me some good physically, mentally, and socially. But it didn't help me achieve the desired goal. As faithfully as I followed all the rules, frankly, I don't think the guy in question ever even gave me a second look.

And that brings up an important point, one that too often gets lost among all the rules and all the pressure: the fact that it's impossible to control another person's thoughts, feelings, attitudes, and attractions. That should be obvious, but in reality, it's something we tend to forget. We can spend the rest of our lives trying to make ourselves over, but still, no one is obligated to find us attractive. Attraction doesn't work that way.

By the Numbers

In this context, Jon Birger's book *Date-Onomics: How Dating Became a Lopsided Numbers Game* points out something very interesting. Birger, a business journalist, looks at the numbers and posits that "It's not that He's Just Not Into You—it's that There Aren't Enough of Him."[9] He explains that at this point in time, there are significantly more college-educated women than men in the United States in general (with some deviation from that norm in a few areas). And the result is that you get a lot of men more interested in playing the field, or even just sitting back and waiting for their ideal, than in making a commitment and settling down. In such an environment, making yourself more attractive to catch a man's eye works about as well as trying to push together the alike poles of two magnets.

In his first chapter, after sharing some statistics that back up his point, Birger writes:

> Think of every grandmother who has shaken her head and announced—exasperated—that she cannot understand why her granddaughter does not have a nice man in her life. [My own paternal grandmother would be included in that group. She used to make these announcements in public, in front of lots of people. Good times.] Think of the aunt at the wedding reception who wonders aloud why there's a table full of young, single women, yet no single men to sit them with. Think of the 30-something single career women in New York, Toronto, or Los Angeles who gather at brunch on Sundays and complain over mimosas that "There are no guys in this town." For these people, this book will finally deliver the tangible proof that will make them smack their hands down on their tables and say, "Aha! See? I KNEW it!"[10]

Birger's research shows the same trends going on in certain religious groups as in the mainstream. (Specifically, he studied two groups, Orthodox Jews and Mormons, but when I had a chance to speak with him, he said that since the publication of his book he had been getting a lot of feedback from Christians, Muslims, and other groups of believers who identified similar trends in their own faith communities.)

There are several Christian leaders who have tried taking single men to task for the pattern of behavior noticed by Birger and others. I touched earlier on such efforts by Mohler and Driscoll. To those leaders I think many of us single women would like to say, with all due respect and appreciation: please stop helping. Much of the time, these efforts simply breed resentment, both against those leaders and against the opposite sex. Some men feel that they're being saddled with an unfair amount of blame for the situation and it makes them angry. Go hunting on the internet for articles and discussions about single men and the church sometime, and you'll get a taste of just how angry. In fact, you might want to wear a flak jacket and a helmet. (I'll get more into that in section 2.)

We women, for our part, sometimes just get sick of the whole situation, and the idea of dropping out of the dating scene altogether grows more and more appealing to many of us. The recent World War I novel *We That Are Left* by Clare Clark offers a helpful and memorable description of this mentality. The dearth of men after that war created a situation in Europe much like the one Birger shows us going through now, and Clark gives us a snapshot of it when she shows one of her main characters going to a postwar dance in London. Jessica Melville has long dreamed of the kind of glittering social life that was standard for her class before the war, but when she finally gets to attend a ball, she quickly discovers that a lot of things have changed.

She had spied him immediately, a tall athletic-looking man of perhaps twenty with thick, dark hair and a mocking smile. . . . He looked restless, despite the smile and the girls that clustered around him, weary and bored. Disregarding the name scribbled on her dance card, Jessica had squeezed through the crowd towards him. As she passed him she knocked his drink with her arm, splashing him with champagne.

"What the . . . ?"

"I'm so awfully sorry," she said, smiling up at him contritely. "How terribly clumsy of me."

His face shrivelled. "For Christ's sake," he hissed and he pushed past Jessica, his elbow catching her roughly in the ribs. In her confusion Jessica redirected her smile at a raw-skinned youth of perhaps fifteen . . . who was leading a girl in a pink dress out onto the dance floor. The boy winked.

"Patience, patience," he muttered as they passed. "Wait your turn."

. . . She had fled to the cloakroom, resting her head against the cool glass. It was only when she opened her eyes that she saw the girl on the chaise lounge. She was wearing a pale green dress . . . and reading a book. Their eyes met in the glass. Neither of them said anything. Jessica washed her hands carefully and dried them. . . . Then, taking a deep breath, she opened the door. The clamour of the party rushed in like floodwater. Behind her the girl in the pale green dress smiled faintly and raised her book.

"Come back soon," she said.[11]

When the old rules don't work, when the old demographics have shifted, when the old standards get you derided as too high-maintenance and too fussy, the girl in the green dress starts to look like the smartest person in the place. The quiet seat in a corner with a book, away from it all, becomes extremely tempting. For more than a few single Christian women, the time comes when it feels better to be alone than to be the one always overlooked, elbowed out of the way, or told "wait your turn."

Ironically, this decision that maybe it's better to be alone looks remarkably like the contentment we've been told to seek—but then, too often, we're scolded for being contented outside of marriage! As Joanna implies, it seems that we're not supposed to feel genuine contentment; we're just supposed to be able to "fake contentment" long enough to trick God into deciding we're ready to be married. To some Christians, genuine extramarital contentment is as bad as extramarital sex.

✦ ✦ ✦

Whether we've been left feeling angry, disheartened, confused, or any other combination of unpleasant feelings, what doesn't help us is making us into projects. Doing that sort of thing to people, whether through manipulation, scolding, or even just well-meant advice, tends to backfire. Single people aren't projects to be fixed. We're fellow brothers and sisters in Christ, making the journey through life alongside the rest of the church, and dealing with a set of circumstances and experiences that take a lot of grace and strength to handle—which can't always be easily fixed with advice, scolding, or rules.

Yes, we need to be sanctified, as all Christians do. And yes, we need guidance and teaching to help us toward that goal. But sanctification doesn't come through following a set of Helpful Rules for Remaking Yourself (and Subsequently Catching a Man/Wooing a Woman). True sanctification comes through the work of the Holy Spirit in us, aided by Bible study, corporate worship, and godly teaching. And sanctification isn't supposed to be a means to an end; it's supposed to be an end in itself.

And true friendship with one's fellow Christians doesn't come through constantly making them feel "less than" or "not good enough" or "not ready to sit at the adult table." It comes from seeing them and loving them as they are. To do this, Christians need to start rethinking some of our views about the way we prioritize marriage and how we handle the fact that marriage is not going to happen for everyone. And above all, Christians need to be reminded how to look at single people simply as *people*.

FOUR

◆ ◆ ◆

SINGLES AS PEOPLE

I would . . . encourage the church to encourage married couples to reach out to fellowship with singles outside of church. Very few couples are open to such a thing.—Erin

Celebrate the lives of the singles around you. Have birthday parties for them. Send them flowers on Valentine's Day. Do talk about the struggles you, your husband, and family are having, but also remember to ask us what is new and exciting or hard in our lives.—Allison

What does it mean to see single people as people? What does this look like, in practical terms? I believe we need to handle it on two levels: the individual level and the structural level. I will get into this more in section 3, but let's take just a few moments here to think about how it might work, on both levels.

On the individual level, it can start small—you might be surprised how small. It can look like making sure single people are greeted at the church doors just as warmly as couples and families are. It can look like chatting with a single churchgoer during the coffee hour after church or small group, asking that person how things are going or how you can pray for him or her this week. It can look like inviting that person to sit with you and your family every week at church. Or asking him or her to lunch sometime. Or inviting him or her to your child's birthday party or school play.

These are little things, of course. But all these little things contribute to the slow and steady building of a real relationship, where you care about each other, listen to each other, and value each other—and that works across marital boundaries just as surely as it does within them.

You don't have to understand everything your single friends are going through. The truth is you *can't* fully understand it, any more than they can understand what you're going through. (A word to the wise: please don't say things like "I didn't get married until I was twenty-six; I know just how hard it is!" to single people in their thirties or forties or fifties. It never goes well.)

Yet that doesn't mean you can't be friends. Just to say this cuts across the cultural grain, I realize. We all seem to be convinced today that the number one requirement to get along with people is for them to be able to identify with every single experience we've had and to comprehend perfectly every facet of our character and personality. Social media has only exacerbated the problem. While it can offer us opportunities to meet, talk, and learn from those different from us, if we're willing to take them, it also offers us the temptation to create a bubble filled with those exactly like ourselves, based on whom we like or follow and whom we choose *not* to like or follow.

So we have a harder time understanding each other. And "you don't understand" becomes an excuse to push each other away. Married people feel they can't talk to us about their lives because we won't understand. Single people hesitate to share our struggles because married people won't understand. And those with children, married or single, too often leave the childless out of their thoughts, conversations, and activities because—sing it if you know the words!—we don't understand.

But it doesn't have to be that way. And it shouldn't. To be thoroughly understood, to talk with someone who's been where you are and really gets it, is a wonderful and valuable thing. But it's not a necessary element of friendship, or even of kindness and respect.

In a women's Facebook group I belong to, a new mother recently posted a link to an article titled "I Want All the Perks of Maternity Leave—without Having Any Kids." The woman interviewed for the story, Meghann Foye, explained that she craved "a sabbatical-like break that allows women and, to a lesser degree, men to shift their focus to the part of their lives that doesn't revolve around their jobs." She called it a "Meternity leave."[1]

Understandably, the new mother in our group, worn out from dealing with an adorable but demanding infant, felt pretty sour about the idea. She felt, with justification, that Foye was entirely missing the point about maternity leave, which is nothing like "a sabbatical-like break" and offers no opportunities for "me time."

But another woman in the group, who had married late, chimed in:

> This reminds me of a joke a few single girlfriends and I used to make about throwing each other "single showers" after we hit

73

age 30 still unmarried. . . . I know these are two very different things, but I will say for those who've experienced marriage or babies, it can seem lame for others to want something super-fluously that seems as necessary as maternity leave or a bridal shower. But God designed marriage and family to imprint us with the need for rhythms, rests, and celebrations. For singles, those milestones aren't there, and it actually DOES feel like you're missing out on something you're designed to partake of. So while I think this "Meternity" is gimmicky, I don't think the desire for it is. I think it accompanies the natural desires for the God-given good gifts of life.[2]

Both women were right. Each had a smart and insightful perspective that was healthy for all of us to hear. (I think the point about milestones, in particular, is an incredibly important one, and I'll be writing more about it later.) If either one of them had been the only voice in the conversation, we all would have missed out, but because each of them brought her different experiences and life stage to bear on a controversial topic, we all had the chance to learn and were better off.

But we only reached the place where this was possible through years of friendship (both online and offline), in-cluding many disagreements and struggles as well as a lot of working together, many productive conversations, and a growing respect for each other.

Different like Me

We need people in our lives who understand us . . . but we also need people who are coming from different backgrounds, stages of life, and points of view. We need these people to help us broaden our perspective, look at life from different angles, and get out of our comfortable shell. And they need us too.

In fact, some of my closest friends have families, and we've learned that this can strengthen our friendships instead of weakening them. It takes work on both sides, but it's work worth doing—work that needs to be done, if we take seriously Christ's commands to love and serve our brothers and sisters. Sometimes they have to be patient with me and overlook my blunders or my thoughtlessness. Sometimes I have to do the same for them. Sometimes I have to realize that they can't make time for me, and vice versa. Making friends across barriers requires a lot of grace from both parties. But as the church of God, isn't grace supposed to be what we're all about?

I realize I'm asking for something significant, and I don't do it lightly. Even the little things take time and effort—time and effort you may not feel you can give. But it's easier if you can find ways to draw single friends into your family life.

My friend Laura made me godmother to all three of her children, sends me their drawings and book reports, and encourages them to send me cards and talk to me on the phone. When I visit them or they visit me, we all hang out and do things together. Instead of taking time away from her family for me, she shares her family with me, and I cherish my relationships with all of them.

Another friend of mine, Jennifer Fulwiler, is a mom of six, a writer, and a radio host who still manages to include single and childless friends in her life. She explained:

> I can't do girls nights out once a week. So I invite my friends—people who have families or people who don't—to just come

have dinner with us. That's a great way that I can get that socialization without maxing out my schedule.

We've cultivated a group of friends with whom our whole family gets along. It's a great way to kill a lot of birds with one stone—we just get the whole families together. Or, if it's someone who doesn't have kids, I'll invite them to come have dinner with the family.[3]

Additionally, you can look for opportunities to work with single people in ministry. This is how I developed a friendship with one of my favorite couples, Bob and Nancy. Bob was for many years the music minister at my former church, where I participated in both choir and instrumentals, and Nancy was the church bookstore manager, so she and I bonded over a shared love of books. We had lots of things in common, and more importantly, both of them have huge hearts and became good friends and mentors to many in the church, both married and single. Their friendships blended seamlessly with their ministries and made their lives (as well as their friends' lives) richer and their work more effective.

You can even bond with fellow Christians in the workplace, though we don't always think of it as an ideal breeding ground for spiritual bonding. Some of my own closest friendships have formed that way. I met Kim at work when she was a divorcée with two kids, and we became good friends; when she married again, I became friends with her new husband, Terry, as well. A few years later she lost Terry in a tragic accident, and many of us who had befriended her through work were there to grieve with her and help her all we could. Through each life stage, and even after we no longer worked in the same place, our friendship has held together, because we have a lot in common, care about each other, and always make room for each other in our lives, no matter what.

This is the kind of friendship that singles need, not the kind of friendship that's based wholly on wanting to swoop in, fix their lives for them, and swoop back out. Please don't get me wrong: the desire to help marriage happen for single people is a good and kind desire—I know that many of us, if not all, are grateful for such help. (My own friends are welcome to set me up any time!) But it can hardly be done by tearing people down. It has to be the kind of effort that flows naturally out of an established friendship, in ways that honor your friend's good qualities and are sensitive to his or her needs and desires. It can't just be a case of "He's breathing and she's breathing—it's a perfect match!" Do that enough times and your single friends will start thinking you don't actually know them at all, or else that you just don't care about who they are and what they're looking for in a partner.

And in any case, even when your single friends appreciate your matchmaking, that's only a very tiny part of the relationships that could and should exist between married people and single people.

The Body of Christ

On the structural level, church leaders can help create environments that aid relationship-building. One way to do this is by restructuring classes, groups, and activities to include both single and married people instead of keeping them apart. While it can be helpful for both single people and married people to have time with others who can relate to their experiences, there's no good reason that the congregation has to keep being segregated by marital status all the time. It's a hindrance to the unity of the body of Christ, reinforcing the false message that we need to spend all our time with those who are just like us, rather than imitating Christ by reaching out across artificial barriers.

Blogger Lindsey Nobles wrote a post called "Church and the Single Girl," and one commenter there, called Kelly, spoke of her own experience, as a single woman, designing the logo and marketing materials for a church that insisted on having the word "family" in everything. Kelly expressed her concerns to her pastor about this, but he "just didn't get it." She concluded, "I spent hours creating all of the marketing materials for my church and all of it felt like they were saying to me, 'Hey, thanks for all your help, but this church really isn't for you. Come back when you are married and grown up.'"[4]

Is your church saying this to single people? Take a look around. How many activities and groups are labeled "Families Only" or "Couples Only," either explicitly or implicitly? What kind of language do your website and your brochures and your bulletins use? What impression do graphics, videos, small group names, and activities give? How many of these voices that Nobles described in her blog post are you hearing in your church:

> The small group leader who suggests four times at the fall kick-off meeting that they just really want this to be convenient for the families . . . the pastor who on Sunday morning casually equates maturity with marriage . . . the conference planner who doesn't fight to find and include single voices— not so that they can talk about singleness per se but so that not all references and stories have to do with marriage and parenting.[5]

The thing is every class, outing, and slogan that bears the label "Families Only" also bears a second label that says "Singles: Keep Out." It may be harder to see if you're in the favored inner circle, but trust me, it's there. And single people are following that instruction—often following it all the way out the church doors.

Even those of us who remain sometimes have trouble speaking out and asking for change. At my former church, every Sunday during the month of December, a different family with young children would be called up to light an Advent candle and talk about what Advent means. It was sweet to watch the parents asking their kids questions and helping them with the answers. It was also painful.

On one level I understood and appreciated that Advent was thus shown to be a meaningful time for parents to teach their kids about the coming of Christ. On another level, it hurt me a little to see that, thanks to this tradition, this seemed to be *all* Advent was. No childless couple or single person was ever called upon to do the important duty of lighting the candle and speaking to the congregation. And though I don't suppose it ever occurred to any of the leaders, that said something to us single and childless people about how the church saw us.

I never spoke up about this to anyone, so maybe it's a little unfair for me to criticize the church for it here. I'm at fault too—maybe more at fault in this case, because I felt like something was wrong but I didn't bring it to the attention of those who could have done something about it. I was so torn over whether I should speak up that I never did. (*You want to speak out against the cute little kids?* a voice in my head kept asking me incredulously. *You want to be the*

Advent Grinch? Really?) Yet if I had taken that risk, maybe I would have helped to change some things in the church that needed to be changed.

Mind you, I'm not saying I would have done a good job at Advent wreath duty myself. It's embarrassing to admit this, but I'm the world's worst at lighting candles. You would not believe it's possible for a sentient adult to be as bad at lighting candles as I am. I would have made a mess of it. (Although it might have helped that at least they had lighters to use, because I'm marginally better with lighters than matches.) But that's not the point. The point is I should have spoken up to make things better, not for myself personally but for all the other single and childless people in the church. To take one baby step toward helping others see us for who we are: full-fledged members of the body of Christ, capable of being fully incorporated into the life of the church.

For the church *can* change its ways in this area. The body of Christ can learn to show the consideration and respect for each of its members—regardless of status—the Bible commands us to show. But to be able to change these things, the church first has to be willing to see them.

So we need to talk in more depth about what, specifically, we're hearing from our pastors and writers on subjects like love, marriage, and singleness. The messages coming from the pulpit and the bookshelf play a crucial role in how we think about and treat our fellow Christians. They also play an absolutely essential role in determining how we got to where we are, with singleness on the rise in the church and with relations breaking down, not just between singles and married people but even between singles themselves.

How We Got Here

We castrate and bid the geldings be fruitful.

C. S. Lewis, *The Abolition of Man*[1]

What messages have single people been receiving from the church in recent years, and how have they shaped the subculture in which single Christians live? To explore answers to these questions is to take a trip to some fairly strange places. To be part of the Christian singles scene these days is to belong to a sort of bizarre world, a fractured reflection of reality where everyone knows how things are *supposed* to work but hardly anyone knows how to make them work that way.

We know quite well that for most people, at most times and in most places, dating and then marriage and then children has been the natural order of things. We've seen people in relationships and marriages all our lives. We've even seen many of our friends and relatives achieve these milestones; we've congratulated them on the beautiful engagement ring, bought the bridesmaid dress and shoes, gone to the bridal showers and, later, the baby showers. And then, very often, we go back home alone, where we "like" all the happy family photos on Facebook and silently wonder if it will ever be our turn.

Because a great number of us will tell you that, for some strange reason, our own attempts at romantic relationships never quite seem to go anywhere. Attempts to attract the attention of the opposite sex very frequently go unrewarded. At church parties, girls and guys gravitate to opposite sides of the room, for all the world like they're at an eighth-grade dance carefully policed by chaperones. For many on the Christian singles scene, dates seem to occur about as often as Halley's Comet.

And when they do occur—when a young Christian man and a young Christian woman manage to go out together and get coffee or lunch or, by some miracle, even dinner—a first date so very often fails to lead to a second date. Men and women drift together, then apart, and any attempt to forge a genuine connection tends to fizzle out before it has a chance to go anywhere. My single friends and I have seen it happen—more than that, we've lived it—over and over and over again.

As for online dating, which we're always being urged to try, the fact is quite a few of us *have* tried it. But that comes with its own set of problems and difficulties, some of which I've already talked about in the previous section. There are success stories, it's true—most of us can number at least a few of those among our own acquaintances—but then there are also horror stories. Lots of them. To share a couple of my own: there was the guy whose table manners were so dreadful that I had to bolt for the ladies' room because I couldn't bear to watch anymore. And then there was the guy who invited me out for appetizers—so he could get away fast in case the date turned out to be a drag, as he informed me after I arrived—and then spent most of the date making crude jokes and suggestive remarks. And those are some of the milder stories out there.

Mostly, though, there are just stories with no ending. For the most part, relationships begun via dating site yield a few emails, maybe a phone call or two, and then fade away.

Many church members are aware of our troubles on the dating front but very few have any clear notion what's behind the situation or what to do about it. Talk to members of some of the older Christian generations about what's going on among the singles, and you'll tend to hear things like this:

"I don't know why they can't just get together and get married!"

"The girls are too picky and the guys are too immature."

"These young women are too independent and too career-focused. They don't make the guys feel needed."

"My daughter wants to get married but just can't seem to find anyone. I don't understand it."

"They're all just too self-centered to get married."

"It's all because of feminism/Disney princesses/too many Jane Austen novels."

"It's all because of pornography/Peter Pan syndrome/too many video games."

On the other hand, talk to single Christians themselves, and here are some of the things you might hear:

I think it hasn't been until the last few years that I haven't been scared to interact with the opposite sex! . . . Guys are supposed to "guard a woman's heart" and girls are supposed to "not be a distraction." So guys walk around feeling like if they are friends with girls, they have to explain that they aren't interested in anything more than being friends. And girls walk around feeling like they can never wear a sundress and that if they call a guy, they are sending the wrong message. All this silliness just creates awkwardness for both sexes, making it almost impossible to merely "be friends" with each other.—Anne

[My] particular branch [of campus ministry] had a very, very strong message to women that we should NOT date but rather should pray and wait for God to bring us a spouse. A lot of not-necessarily-unhealthy relationships ended because people "needed to focus on God right now." There was a big disparity between being in a relationship with another person and a relationship with God. . . . It led to a lot of frustrated women and a lot of men who were content to just drift while "waiting on the Lord." It also created an unhealthy environment of expectation, that is: "Only the spiritually mature get married." So then you had frustrating situations where "Well, so-and-so is only HERE in their walk with God and THEY'RE getting married."—Ashley

On messages that the church sends about dating and relationships:

You should be married.
You should not get to know your potential spouse.
Sex outside of marriage is wrong.—Eric *(emphasis mine)*

Or as Christian writer Annie F. Downs tells us in her book *Let's All Be Brave*:

> You want me to get ugly honest about what it can be like to be a single Christian woman when you don't want to be single? Sometimes you don't think you can do another day.[2]

Things look a little different from the front lines, don't they?

It's true that many worldly factors, leaking from the secular culture into the church, have played a major role in the current state of affairs. I don't mean to dismiss that aspect of things. Unless we're Old Order Amish, the society we live in is bound to color our attitudes and ideas to some extent. Many of us have, knowingly or unknowingly, adopted relational ideas and practices from the larger culture, ideas and practices that aren't always healthy or God-honoring.

But it's also true that the church itself has played a very real and deeply significant role in this situation—and that's what I want to focus on right now. Albeit with the best intentions in the world, the church has created a culture that simultaneously pressures singles to get married and makes it very difficult for them to do so.

To understand more about this culture, the reasoning behind it, and the results of it, we have to go back a couple of decades. We can't fully understand the relationship between single Christians and the larger church, and how it needs to change, until we've gained a basic understanding of what the church has been teaching us and why—of the place that the church has given us to inhabit, if you will, and how living in that place has shaped our faith, our relationships, and our lives. Only when we've explored all this can we start learning how to transform this often strange and contorted landscape into a place where single Christians find it easier to live full lives and form healthy relationships.

FIVE

◆ ◆ ◆

THE MAN IN THE HAT

If you belonged to an evangelical church in the 1990s, you'll likely remember a certain book cover featuring a man with his face mostly hidden by a hat. For a long time, in fact, the man in the hat was pretty much everywhere you looked. That classy-looking, old-fashioned cover image gave the book a reassuring vibe for a wide range of Christian readers. Here, it indicated, was something solid, something safe, a set of values that harked back to the days of good, lasting marriages.

The book was, of course, *I Kissed Dating Goodbye* by Joshua Harris, who wrote it when he was just twenty-one years old. It has sold more than a million copies, going into a second edition in 2003.[1] It was read by youth groups and taught in Sunday school classes (including mine). It came out at a time when a growing number of Christians were worrying about disturbing trends, not just in mainstream culture but in our own ranks: climbing divorce rates, teen pregnancy, more and more young Christians ignoring their church's teachings on sexuality to do things their own way. And, therefore, the book found an audience primed and ready to turn it into a publishing phenomenon. As blogger "David B." recalls:

> You couldn't go to any retreat, meeting, or whatever, without hearing about this book, and its philosophy, as if it really was the gospel. New converts to Christianity I knew often owned multiple copies of the book and would pass it out to anyone and everyone they met. People would go to dinner and a movie with someone of the opposite sex, but bend over backwards to call it anything but a "date," because they had been taught, and believed, that "dating" is sinful.[2]

But as trends often do, *I Kissed Dating Goodbye* and the courtship movement that surrounded it sparked a backlash—one that lasts to this day. Just mentioning the book's title can cause strong, almost visceral reactions among a certain demographic. Here are a few thoughts on the book from some of my interviewees:

> *I have long said that* I Kissed Dating Goodbye *is the single most harmful thing to have ever happened to the Christian dating scene.*—Ashley

> I Kissed Dating Goodbye *is not my favorite book, that's for sure! It came out around the time when I should have been starting to date. It made dating too complicated. Why can't dating be a girl and guy getting to know each other over Coke? . . . And then getting to know another guy over a Coke, and another, with no pressure or mixed signals?*—Lynn

> *I felt [the book] was fundamentally flawed. It seemed that the author redefined the word "dating" to mean*

"dating abuses," thoroughly confusing courtship and providing barriers to marriage.—Eric

I really think in a lot of ways the books by Josh Harris, the Myers [authors of Of Knights and Fair Maidens*], and the Ludys [authors of* When God Writes Your Love Story*] have been harmful. I don't think they mean to imply this, but I think readers often take away the idea that if they live the life of purity and faithfully follow where the Lord is leading them to go, it will result in finding Prince Charming.*—Allison

And here's writer Tim Holland, in a piece poignantly titled "I Kissed Dating Goodbye, Where Did It Go?"

Looking back on my decision not to date until I was "ready for marriage," it is evident that this course has led me to become a bit of a cripple when it comes to approaching women. . . . I just wish I had more to show for the past 10 years of my failed romantic life than a few quick flings, an extensive knowledge of the Star Trek universe and the deep brokenness that weighs heavily upon my heart. While putting the brakes on dating was good wisdom for some of my more sexed-up peers, I could really have used a good kick in the pants to throw me into gear.[3]

What was in this book that caused such a fuss?

For a long time Harris and his defenders argued that there wasn't anything at all—that his words were simply being widely misinterpreted. But when a book helps to create a whole set of beliefs by which a generation of Christians is taught to live—when its message is that widespread and that effectual—it seems safe to say that the majority interpretation is probably the correct one. As C. S. Lewis observes in his book *An Experiment in Criticism*, if a vast number of readers are all getting the same thing out of a book, it should tell you something about what the book is really like.[4]

With that in mind, let's take a quick look at what really is in *I Kissed Dating Goodbye*—and how, for better or worse, the book and the mentality that it helped to spread have affected more than one generation.

First of all, it should be made clear at the outset that the book is part of something much bigger than itself. The principles of *I Kissed Dating Goodbye* grew out of principles practiced in Harris's church, many of which in turn had been loosely adapted from the likes of Bill Gothard and his Institute in Basic Life Principles.[5] Gothard may not be a name you know, but if you're at all familiar with the Duggar family, you've seen something of the teachings he's been espousing for decades. Gothard and his followers are known for insisting on highly rigid standards of dress, discipline, and lifestyle.[6]

Joshua Harris toned down a lot of Gothard's more extreme ideas and positions, but the basic underlying principles in regard to dating/courting were very similar. And with his book's success, a whole movement grew up around it, in a ripple effect that ultimately left hardly any evangelical church in the United States unaffected.

So keep in mind that the trends and ideas I'm going to discuss in this and subsequent chapters can't all be pinned on one book. But that book encapsulates most if not all of the distinguishing characteristics of the movement, and that movement has had an indelible effect not just on the Christian singles scene but on the church in general.

The first chapter of *I Kissed Dating Goodbye* opens with Harris vividly describing a dream that one of his correspondents told him about—a dream in which all the other girls her fiancé had ever dated were standing with them at the altar as they got married. Harris then applies this scenario to his own dating life: "I'm still aware of the consequences of my selfishness. I gave my heart away too many times. And I took from girls what wasn't mine."[7] As he will later make clear, he's talking not about physical acts but emotional ones.

The altar scenario—which, as I recall, became a potent and much-discussed symbol among the generation raised on Harris's book—sets the tone for what follows. That's important to keep in mind, because as the book's defenders are always pointing out, Harris never comes right out and says that dating is sinful. He really doesn't. He just uses words and images like these to make it look very, very bad. You *could* date, of course—it's not *technically* wrong—but don't you want to be better than that? Don't you want to be as holy as you possibly can? And given all the problems and temptations that plague people in dating relationships, isn't it obvious that dating keeps people from being as holy as they possibly can?

Give the man some credit—it takes a gifted writer to be able to pull off that kind of sleight of hand.

Instead of dating, Harris advocates for a system of courtship that includes lots of going out together in groups (and very little time spent alone), families and friends and church leaders getting heavily involved (often the father is asked for permission to court his daughter), no kissing until marriage, and so forth. Of course, this means that a given couple will have lots of aid in fighting sexual temptation. Additionally, it means—or at least it was supposed to mean—that they can get to know each other free from the pressure to get physical too quickly and thus build a lasting marriage on a solid foundation. Further, it means—or it was supposed to mean—that they can "guard their hearts" (a common catchphrase among courtship advocates, based on Proverbs 4:23) against getting too emotionally attached too quickly and thus spare themselves and others a lot of pain.

But it also means a lot of other things—things that Joshua Harris and all those parents and pastors and Sunday school teachers promoting his book and pushing the courtship movement didn't realize at the time.

I'd like to talk about what it meant for two young couples in particular, both of them with close ties to Harris.

Bethany and Sam

Bethany Patchin was the "It Girl" of the courtship movement in the late '90s and early '00s. As a bright young Christian college student and a devotee of *I Kissed Dating Goodbye*, Bethany wrote an enthusiastic article called "(Don't) Kiss Me" that went viral even before such a thing as "going viral" really existed. Here's an excerpt from it:

> I'm a sophomore in college with virgin lips. A few months after turning 16, I vowed to keep my "bow" tied until a man promises to commit himself to the whole package. My first kiss will be from my husband on our wedding day. Yes, that's quite a progression, from an inexpert kiss at the altar to the complete unwrapping of the wedding night—believe me, my friends have pointed that out. Then again, Adam and Eve managed to figure everything out in a day. . . .

God asks different things of different people. My point is not that everyone should take a vow against premarital kissing. My challenge is that this generation of Christians would take a deeper look at something we treat so lightly. That we would take the initiative in saving something so precious for the right time and person—that we would pray about grasping what Solomon meant when he said there is a time to embrace and a time to refrain from embracing. That we would understand how intricately kissing is involved with Jesus and that we would ask Him how we can better obey His commands for purity.[8]

With this, Bethany Patchin both launched a prolific writing career and added a significant amount of fuel to the courtship movement. She also got a letter from a young Christian man named Sam Torode, who wasn't fully convinced she was right and wanted to argue the point. Just like a meet-cute in an old movie, argument led to romance—and in this context, there was pretty much only one way that romance was going to end up. Bethany, age nineteen, and Sam, twenty-four, were married just a year and four months after her article had been published.

And wouldn't you know it, by that time, Sam had come around to Bethany's point of view on the "no kissing before marriage" thing, and also on the whole courtship thing in general. He came around so completely, in fact, that he wrote the foreword to the second edition of *I Kissed Dating Goodbye*.

"To my surprise," Sam wrote in that foreword, "I discovered *I Kissed Dating Goodbye* isn't really about dating at all. Instead, it's a book about following Christ and what that means for *all* of our relationships with others—whether

romantic or not. . . . Indeed, my own story proves that foregoing casual dating (and even kissing) just might be the thing
that brings you and your spouse together."[9]

Sam and Bethany were the perfect poster children for the
courtship movement, with a wholesome, romantic, by-the-
book (literally) relationship that played out in front of an
admiring young Christian audience. They were living examples of just how good life, and especially romance, could
be when you followed the rules. And after they were married,
they continued to write about romance, marriage, and sex
in a Christian context, including an anti–birth control book
called *Open Embrace*.

Ten years and four children later, Bethany and Sam divorced. As it turned out, their courtship had not prepared
them for the stresses and strains of marriage or taught them
the best and healthiest ways to interact. What they went
through in those ten years of marriage, Bethany later told a
New York Times reporter, was so "intense" that it not only
broke them apart but also flung them completely out of their
conservative Christian world.

> Today, neither Ms. Patchin nor Mr. Torode is part of the an-
> ticontraception community, nor conservative Christianity. . . .
> "Where I'm at now, it's confusing," Ms. Patchin said.
> "One day I am like, 'Sure, God exists and loves all of us,' and
> the next day I am like, 'No, I don't think so.' I think that's
> healthy. Agnosticism is a healthy part of any good faith."[10]

Both Bethany and Sam have disavowed their writings on
courtship. The website where Bethany published "(Don't)
Kiss Me" and many other articles has taken her work down,
though it can still be accessed elsewhere on the web. But

Sam's foreword is still part of *I Kissed Dating Goodbye*, as the 2003 edition is still on bookstore shelves today.

Megan and Kerrin

This young couple was featured in Joshua Harris's follow-up book, *Boy Meets Girl: Say Hello to Courtship* (2000). This was a book designed to help Christian young adults figure out the practicalities of getting to know someone romantically when dating was no longer considered a wise or holy option.

Megan Kauflin and Kerrin Russell were good friends of Harris—in fact, Megan was the worship leader's daughter at the church where Harris was then the pastoral intern and later became the senior pastor—so he had a front-row view of their courtship. In a chapter called "Courtship Is a Community Project," he writes about how, "when Megan found out from her dad that Kerrin was interested in her, she almost turned him down. He just wasn't her type."[11]

But Megan's family and friends convinced her that a good courtship should be less about attraction and more about the character of the man who was interested in her. They told her things like "You can't trust your affections, but you can rely on love and character." Joshua Harris quotes Megan herself as writing in her journal, "I guess I thought I deserved better. It's just foolish pride. . . . My ideals were all wrong."[12]

Harris adds, "Megan's journal shows how God used a friend's words to gently prod her in the right direction. Megan was confused. She felt overwhelmed by her emotions. Like someone stumbling through a fog-shrouded valley, she needed others standing on the hills above the valley to call out to her with guidance."[13] And so at last, surrounded by the Christian family and friends who had given them so much guidance, Megan and Kerrin were married.

About eleven or twelve years and five children later, they divorced. She's now remarried and he lives overseas.[14]

"This Was Not the Deal"

Now obviously, plenty of couples who went the courtship route have gotten married and stayed married. But these two high-profile examples, as well as a number of lower-profile examples, suggest that the supposedly rock-solid stability offered by the courtship culture might not be quite as solid as it appeared. As Thomas Umstattd Jr., founder of PracticalCourtship.com, observed:

> Each year I waited for courtship to start working and for my homeschool friends to start getting married. It never happened. Most of them are still single. Some have grown bitter and jaded. Then couples who did get married through courtship started getting divorced. I'm talking the kind of couples who first kissed at their wedding were filing for divorce.
>
> This was not the deal!
>
> The deal was that if we put up with the rules and awkwardness of courtship now we could avoid the pain of divorce later. The whole point of courtship was to have a happy marriage, not a high divorce rate.[15]

The way of thinking that Umstattd describes was absolutely pervasive in the evangelical church for years, and we're still feeling the effects of it today, which is why I'm spending so much time on it here. Though it wasn't actually guaranteed in so many words, many people who remember those days, like Umstattd, will tell you that the courtship movement was grounded in a sort of unspoken assurance that this kind of relationship-building was Christians' defense against both premarital sex and divorce.

But as it turned out, even some of the highest elites in the courtship movement couldn't make it work. And if it's true for them, how much truer it is for many ordinary young Christian men and women who found these ideals and practices pulling them apart instead of drawing them together? De-emphasizing attraction, allowing young people little time or space to actually get to know each other, making them concentrate heavily on just a couple aspects of their relationship, teaching them to doubt or question their own instincts all the time and constantly rely on the advice of those outside the relationship, encouraging young women in particular to ignore their own feelings and instincts—is it really so surprising that this wasn't the formula for long-lasting marriage it was meant to be?

◆　◆　◆

Let me say something that may surprise you: I'm not holding Joshua Harris solely, or even primarily, responsible for this state of affairs. For one thing, he didn't force anyone to read his book or follow its precepts; and for another, he was very young and very idealistic when he wrote it.[16] It was the adults around him who should have known better. Many of us have utopian ideals at the age of twenty-one; very few of us—thank God—are encouraged to have those ideals packaged and promoted in nearly every evangelical church in America.

The thing that must always be remembered about utopia— though generation after generation seems to keep forgetting it—is that it's not real. It's an ideal of perfection that simply can't work in a fallen world, where no human being is perfect. And history tells us that the attempt to bring it about usually does more harm than good.

When young Joshua Harris's vision of utopia caught on in the evangelical church, there weren't enough adults standing back and saying, "Wait a minute—do we really want a kid teaching other kids how to create happy, healthy, lasting relationships? Isn't that a bit like the blind leading the blind?" Instead, the adults got caught up in the trend. The evangelical church may preach fervently against too much reliance on traditions, but, let's face it, we dearly love our trends—which I would argue are merely a modern version of traditions.

So Harris's youth was sold as a feature, not a bug. Everyone got so excited over finding someone who could get the young people's attention, someone from the kids' own generation who could speak their own language, that they forgot to consider whether that was really a good idea.

And we're still dealing with the consequences today.

SIX

◆ ◆ ◆

COURTSHIP CRAZY

I feel like the church over-spiritualizes relationships, and it hasn't been until the last few years that I've realized I absorbed this mentality but don't agree with it. You are supposed to "wait for the Lord's timing" or "let Him reveal the one He has for you." Then, when you do meet someone, you need to court or "make your intentions known" or something to that effect. While God definitely puts different things on different people's hearts, I don't think there is only one way to meet someone and begin a relationship, and I think a lot of this is unnecessarily old-fashioned and not necessarily biblical.—Anne

The advice given to me constantly as a young single was "Do nothing—God will bring her along." Imagine putting that advice to job-hunting.—Ed

To get a thorough picture of the courtship movement and its effects, let's look at a few other books that Christian women in my generation were encouraged to read and take to heart, and talk briefly about the messages we took away from them. (Some of these, particularly the first two, were also aimed at young men. But I'm focusing primarily on what things were like for young women, as that, of course, is the only area in which I have firsthand experience. Keep in mind, though, that the boys were getting the male equivalent of what we girls were getting.)

Boy Meets Girl

I've already mentioned Harris's follow-up book, *Boy Meets Girl*, the one that was supposed to translate the lofty ideals of *I Kissed Dating Goodbye* into practical terms. Here's a sample of that practicality, from chapter 4, in which the author promises to "use one couple's story to illustrate principles that can help you with the *how* and *when* and *with whom* questions of courtship."

- The boy in this story (David) decided he wanted to pursue the girl (Claire). He prayed about it, asked himself seven questions (1. "Am I prepared to lead my wife spiritually and serve her in every way? 2. Do I have proven character, and am I growing in godliness?" etc.), prayed about the questions, answered them affirmatively, and called Claire's father for permission to approach Claire.
- Upon hearing that David was interested in her, Claire—who was *not* interested in him, except as a friend—pitched a fit. A literal fit. ("Throwing herself down on

the couch, she pounded the arm with both fists and yelled hysterically . . .") It seems Claire was interested in someone else, but since that young man didn't consider himself ready for marriage yet, Claire's father had put that relationship indefinitely "on hold."

- Nonetheless, Claire grudgingly agreed to go out with David. Then she didn't speak to him for two months. Then she felt bad and apologized for not treating him "like a brother."

- "David talked to his pastor, Kenneth. . . . 'Dave, I think you've made an idol out of marriage,' Kenneth told him. . . . 'Look at your response to her lack of interest. You grew bitter; you got angry. That leads me to think that you want marriage too much.'"

- Two years later, having given up on her "on hold" guy, Claire had new feelings for David: "Before it had always been, 'Here's the guy I want!' But this time I thought, 'Here's a man I could follow.'"

- David still had feelings for Claire. But he decided to wait and let God tell him who to pursue. But then his parents "challenged him not to hold back because of fear," so he assumed this was The Voice of God and decided to pursue Claire again. This time, she said yes to courtship.[1]

Let me reiterate: the point of this labyrinthine epic was to help *keep* people from getting confused. All this—the constant second-guessing of one's own emotions and instincts, appeals for outside help, and going back and forth on everything from how much one should want marriage to whom one should want to marry—was supposed to provide crystal-clear guiding principles to show you exactly how to progress from singleness to marriage. This was a relationship blueprint.

And people wonder why so many single Christian adults have so much trouble building romantic relationships.

I . . . dated a guy . . . who got stuck at the youth group stage. He didn't want to kiss until his wedding day, and though I respected that, he couldn't articulate why. . . . He just "knew" it was something he was "supposed" to do. I feel like, especially to those who are just entering the relational life stage, the church really misses the mark by focusing far too much on what not *to do. I feel like if, instead, the church came alongside young adults and taught them how to form and maintain healthy relationships instead of telling them* not *to have bad ones, it would be far more productive.*—Ashley

When God Writes Your Love Story

In the 2009 book *When God Writes Your Love Story*, Eric and Leslie Ludy use their own love story to teach that if you put God in charge of your love life, He will shower you with every blessing you ever wanted. No need to date around—God will point out the right one at the right time, so why even think of running the physical and emotional risks of dating? As for singleness, no worries—that won't *really* happen to you! Give God total control, keep yourself pure for your future spouse, and that God-guaranteed knight or princess will be plopped down in front of you, just as sure as the sunrise.

Well, *almost* as sure. Eric does acknowledge another possibility in one of his chapters: "Even if we *never* get married, *nothing* we do in guarding our hearts, filtering our thoughts, and cherishing our future spouse by the way we live will be wasted."[2]

Just ponder that sentence for a minute. You should cherish your future spouse . . . even if you don't *have* a future spouse. Basically, you should live for someone who might not exist.

Obviously, syntax issues aside, the Ludys are trying to express the idea that we're really supposed to live pure lives out of obedience to God. But it's more than a little ironic that, in a book that purports to be all about "giving God the pen" to write your love story, as Leslie puts it in one of her chapters, the focus is so much more on living for one's future spouse than on living for God.[3]

After all, Leslie writes:

> I pictured myself trusting God with this precious area of my life, only to end up sitting in a long, gray, tentlike dress, staring forlornly out the window and rocking my life away in a rocking chair. . . . Looking back, I laugh at such a thought. That was before I learned what a true romantic God is. If I had only known what He had planned for me . . . I never would have doubted for a minute![4]

In other words, God wanted what she wanted for herself, even more than she wanted it, so there was never really any danger that she might have to go through life alone—which, she seems to imply, would have been a fate worse than death. For anyone who's experienced single adulthood for more than, say, five or six years, the Ludys' book is far more conducive to frustration than to inspiration.

Girls Gone Wise in a World Gone Wild

In *Girls Gone Wise in a World Gone Wild*, published in 2010, Mary A. Kassian helpfully clarifies the role of women in a courtship culture—including teaching us that a girl who does anything different from what that culture dictates is a hussy. Think I'm being too harsh? Consider this:

> The phone was ringing. Katy was calling for the eighth time that evening. She had called five times the evening before and nine times the evening before that. I knew what this seventh grader wanted . . . to speak to my youngest son, Jonathan. Instead of beckoning him to the phone, I normally took a message, so he could call her back at his leisure. My standard reply to her inquiry if she could speak to him was, "I'll give him the message and have him call you back."
>
> Which he did. When it suited him. But that wasn't good enough for Katy. She was getting irritated that I was interfering with her desire to cajole my son into jumping through her hoops. . . .
>
> I remember thinking about how aggressive young girls had become. It used to be that the girls waited for the guys to call them. A female phoning a male was very forward and inappropriate. Social etiquette stipulated that the male was the pursuer. But the feminist movement changed all that. Women became the pursuers. . . . Females have morphed into hawkish predators. For a mom trying to raise godly sons, it's scary out there![5]

After telling Katy's story, Kassian proceeds to tell "Heidi's" story (pursued a man, ended up with a "deadweight" for a husband) and then the story of her own daughter-in-law (never took any initiative at all, got a wonderful husband). And then she revisits Katy again (if she doesn't mend her ways, she'll probably end up with a "wimp").

There's no middle ground here. Kassian does temper all this with "Is it wrong for [a woman] to initiate from time to time? No."[6] But at this point, that disclaimer carries about as much weight as Joshua Harris vividly describing that horrible dream of all the past loves at the altar and then saying that dating's not *really* wrong. Kassian's real message has been delivered, and very effectively at that.

Granted, the girl's actions as Kassian describes them were indeed out of line. A parent has every right to be annoyed with a kid who won't quit calling her house. But that's just it: Katy was a kid. Kids do a lot of foolish, impulsive things they shouldn't. It's all part of growing up and learning to navigate the world around them. But to have this immature twelve-year-old girl held up as an example of why it's wrong for a woman to ask out a man . . . well, it makes it pretty clear what Kassian thinks of such women.

And frankly, it made me feel a little sorry for Katy, despite her aggravating behavior. If Christian ladies were labeling her a predator at the age of twelve, I hate to think about what her experience of church, if she had any such experience, must have been like.

The upshot is we got the message that women are supposed to fit a particular mold, men are supposed to fit a particular mold, and disaster ensues whenever someone attempts to break out of the mold. It's a message that—like so many other messages coming out of the courtship culture—allows for very little freedom, leniency, or relaxation in relationships between Christian men and women.

Passion and Purity

Elisabeth Elliot, the widow of martyred missionary Jim
Elliot, expresses a similar sentiment even more strongly in
Passion and Purity, one of the most popular relationship
books for Christian girls when I was growing up. First published in 1984, Elliot's book is one of the heavyweights of
the courtship movement. (Joshua Harris wrote the foreword
to the 2002 edition, lauding the book for its influence on
his thinking about romantic relationships.) Here's some of
what she had to say about male and female roles in courtship and dating.

> "Be careful," I say to the woman [who wants to ask a man
> out]. "Don't put him in an indefinable position. Have you
> considered the paradigms and symbols? Does the word *mod-
> esty* ring any bells with you? Is *reserve* an outmoded word
> now? If you should marry Al in the end, would you (would
> he?) want to live with the knowledge that you went after him?
> He might resent you for snaring him. You might despise him
> for allowing you to."
>
> "It was worth the risk," some will say. "We're both glad
> it worked out that way." I imagine they are the sort who will
> say that women have a right to go to war and no right to be
> protected. I prefer not to get into the ring with those who
> take that line of thought.[7]

Now, please hear me: the last thing I want to do is dis-
parage Elisabeth Elliot, who was a great Christian, a great
lady, and far braver and stronger than I will ever be. I have
enormous respect for her and her accomplishments. But as
I said earlier in this book, even the bravest and strongest
human beings are still only human and, as such, are prone

to mistakes. And I'm afraid the passage I've quoted above demonstrates that inescapable truth.

Because I have to tell you, in all honesty, you could break your leg trying to follow Elliot's leap of logic here.

Leave aside (although it's difficult) the mystifying idea that it's only a short step from asking a man out to advocating placing females in combat roles and consider this question: Why does a woman's asking a man out constitute "snaring" him? If both parties are open and honest with each other, and resist game-playing and manipulation, where does the snaring come in?

This is especially confusing because, woven in among her admonitions to girls to remain quiet, passive, and demure, is the story of how Elliot herself was honest, straightforward, and upfront about her feelings during her own courtship with Jim Elliot. But I think perhaps that in writing this and other books on the subjects of courtship and womanhood, Elisabeth Elliot was so eager to promote what she saw as the ideal biblical role for a woman that she may not have fully realized she was offering conflicting messages. And she's not the only one who does this.

Get Married

You may recall that I mentioned *Get Married* in chapter 1. Candice Watters, another Christian writer (and a former editor for both Bethany Patchin and myself), appears to offer a workable option for women in her book—at first. She talks about how her professor's wife encouraged her to "pull a Ruth," to emulate the Old Testament heroine who took rather drastic, though not immoral, measures to encourage a man to propose.

In her own attempt to win a man's heart, Watters started out by inviting him to a dinner party at her house, then by spending lots of time with him, and then finally "[laying] it all on the line":

> [I said,] "Steve, I want to get married and I hope it's to you. But if it's not, then we need to stop spending all this time together. Otherwise, no one else will ask me out—they all think we're dating."[8]

Steve stepped up to the plate, they got married, and the story ended happily. But is Watters recommending that other women follow her example? As a matter of fact, no.

> What I've learned [since then] has significantly changed my ideas about the bold pursuit of a man. . . .
> I guess I had brought a few too many modern sensibilities to my reading of the ancient story, wanting to make Ruth into one of the original examples of girl power. I was so inspired by the way she made good of a bad situation that I missed two key points: it would have been better had she been under the covering of a strong father figure, and she didn't "go after" just anyone.[9]

At this point I can practically hear a whole chorus of her female readers begging, *Please, no! Don't walk it back! Don't tell your success story and then add, "But I was wrong, so don't do it that way."* For those of us who want to be married, reading something like this makes us feel like a kid who's watching another kid climb up to a tree house and then pull the ladder up after her so we can't follow.

To me, this passage reads as if Candice Watters—with the purest motives, like so many other Christian writers—has looked back at her own love story and decided that it should have been more Christian. (Maybe she's even worried that she "snared" her husband!) But why, exactly? She and Steve were, and are, good, God-fearing, God-honoring people. They sought God's will for their romance and their lives. They practiced celibacy until marriage. Why the impulse to self-correct?

Is it, perhaps, that we've unwittingly allowed or even encouraged the goal to change—that as important as it is to achieve a happy, healthy, Christ-centered marriage, some see it as equally important to jump through all the "Christian" hoops to get there? Is marriage somehow less valid or less God-honoring if we don't follow a certain set of rules or system of beliefs to achieve it—and, especially in the case of women, if we were too active in getting there or if we placed too much emphasis on our own ideals, goals, values, and feelings?

That's the impression many of us single Christians were given—and as you might guess, it can be terribly intimidating.

SEVEN

◆ ◆ ◆

PRESSURE
AND PARALYSIS

I feel that there is a bit of a fear of men mixing with women in the singles groups. I am not sure why. I think promoting fellowship and friendship without pressure of dating might help. . . . For example, if a guy and girl are hanging out, people assume things right away. This kind of prevents fellowship and conversation due to social awkwardness.—Bea

There's a reason I've spent so much time examining the works that have helped create the courtship culture. I humbly suggest that before the evangelical church points the finger of blame at the secular culture, or at single Christians themselves, for increasing rates of singleness within the church, it needs to acknowledge its own role. There's no avoiding the fact that, desperate to protect us from all the bad things that can happen to people in dating relationships, the evangelical church effectively tied our hands. It taught us to be passive, to sit still and overanalyze everything and wait . . . and then it wonders why we can't just get on with it.

Don't just take my word for it. Over the years, Joshua Harris himself has come to realize there's a problem. In November 2005, Harris preached a two-part sermon, the first part of which was titled "Courtship, Shmourtship: What Really Matters in Relationships," at Covenant Life Church in Gaithersburg, Maryland, where he was then senior pastor. Here's an excerpt:

> As we have talked as pastors, as we have communicated to different singles, asked them questions and observed the way in which men and women who are single relate in Covenant Life Church, we have observed—and this is not true of all the singles, but some in our midst—a lack of freeness between men and women in cultivating friendships. You could describe this as a standoffishness, as being overly reserved, even a certain level of uptightness. . . .
>
> See, I want mature men in this church not to feel scared about initiating friendship with women. I think there's been some confusion in this regard, and so I'd like to clear it up. I want you to read my lips, write this down, you're hearing this straight from the courtship guru's mouth: It is okay for brothers and sisters to go out to lunch together.[1]

Ten years later—as I was working on this book—Harris revealed in an NPR interview that he had gone even further in the reevaluating process:

> It's so easy to latch on to a formula. You know, you do these things and you'll be great. You'll be safe and you'll be protected and you'll be whatever.

And I just don't think that's the way life works. I don't think that's the way the life of faith works. And so when we try to overly control our own lives or overly control other people's lives, I think we end up harming people. And . . . I think that that's part of the problem with my book.[2]

The man who literally wrote the book on standoffishness between the sexes has finally come to see why it wasn't such a good idea. I appreciate his honest self-evaluation, but the consequences are still playing out in church culture, and even in wider culture, all these years later.

Blogger Darcy Anne Saffer is one woman who was raised on the teachings of Harris and others about "emotional purity" and "guarding one's heart." She's married now (and no longer considers herself a Christian), but she writes that those teachings still linger in her mind and heart, with unforeseen effects:

Where others see nothing wrong, I am suspicious of every look, every situation, every witty exchange. I am still uncomfortable hugging one of my best friends who is a guy. Because we were never to hug or have physical contact, even innocent, with a guy. Voices in my head scream "defrauder!" just by giving a friend a quick hug. I feel ill at ease sometimes even talking to other men. Oh, they never notice. Because I'm really good at pushing those feelings away and acting "normal." But I am bothered by my reaction to everyday situations. We were taught never ever ever to be alone with a guy. Because it could look bad. He could be tempted. You might start thinking impure thoughts. You might even *gasp* flirt!

I was trying to explain this to my friend and it came out sounding so . . . crazy and embarrassing. I told her if she was to walk out of the room, leaving me and her husband in the same room, my first reaction would be one of panic. *"This might look bad . . . what if he talks to me . . . what if someone else sees us . . . what is he thinking?"*[3]

If that's not a recipe for standoffishness and uptightness, I don't know what is. It's not a bad thing to avoid the appearance of evil—the Bible instructs us to do so (1 Thess. 5:22). But if a woman can't even stand next to a man in a room without breaking out in hives for fear that she's giving that appearance, something is off. It's all part and parcel of the hyperstrict, hyperlegalistic singles culture the church has created—the kind of culture that, I submit, is not what Christ had in mind for His followers.

And how about the guys? What is it like for them? Writer Ross Boone puts it this way:

> Even after a few dates, some women want to know if we're really in it or not—if we're willing to commit to the next level. And suddenly the stakes have been raised. In Christian sub-culture it can seem like every man, at every point in the relationship, is supposed to know the answer to this one single question: "Are you pursuing her for marriage? Can you imagine her as your wife?"
>
> In truth, sometimes even answering the question "Do you like her like that or not?" can be overwhelming when you're just getting to know someone.[4]

Christians do still continue to get married and have children, of course—some of them by following the rules of the courtship culture (even an inherently flawed idea can sometimes work), others by managing to find a way around those rules, and still others by having managed to grow up in churches where they weren't especially influential. But at the same time, more and more young Christians are remaining single, very often against their will. Something has shifted. Looking at the way so many of us were raised and trained, one can only ask, is it any wonder?

I was fortunate, myself; my family never bought into courtship culture. My mother has never been one for church trends, no matter how extra-super-holy they were supposed to make you, and my father would have fallen over laughing if I'd ever attempted to put him in charge of my love life. The courtship culture simply wasn't their scene.

But I was fortunate only up to a point. As Susan Olasky observes, "Even Christians who don't like [Joshua Harris's] book feel forced to color within the lines Harris drew—'courtship' is best—because of his influence on so many of the other students in their social milieu."[5]

In other words, when most of your prospective suitors have had their thinking shaped by courtship culture, your own life is going to be affected by it whether you like it or not. Like a chemical that leaks into the ground and infiltrates the drinking water of an entire community, this culture left hardly a family in the evangelical church untouched. Some families embraced it wholeheartedly, to the point where they'd never even think of letting their kids try any other way of conducting a romantic relationship, and looked down on families who didn't go so far. But even many families that didn't buy into the courtship culture at all saw their children get caught up in it.

Bethany Patchin was one such person. She said in her *New York Times* interview, "My parents . . . were pretty middle-ground evangelicals. So I kind of rebelled by being more conservative. That was my identity."[6] Thomas Umstattd Jr. was another. He recalls:

My grandparents would often ask why I wasn't dating in high school. I explained what courtship was and quoted Joshua Harris, chapter and verse. Their response surprised me.

"I don't think courtship is a smart idea," my grandfather said.

"How can you tell who you want to marry if you aren't going out on dates?" my grandmother wondered every time the topic came up. I tried to convince them but to no avail. They both obstinately held to the position that courtship was a foolish idea.

Well, what did they know? They were public schooled. I ignored their advice on relationships, preferring to listen to the young people around me who were passionate advocates of courtship.[7]

Lauren Wilford offers this overview of the phenomenon:

While the practice of "biblical courtship" itself did not penetrate to Christian culture at large, the messages underlying it soon became ubiquitous. Courtship proper—in which a young man pursues a young woman under the strict supervision and guidance of her fathers, earthly and heavenly—was (and is) practiced by a small, passionate core of very traditionalist Christians. It was unapologetically archaic, easy to write off as eccentric, and not something that the average evangelical family was ready to buy wholesale.

But the books that courtship advocates wrote became a phenomenon in Christian culture at large, exerting enough pressure to profoundly shift evangelical discourse about young men, women, and relationships. Thus courtship culture ascended.[8]

It's a dangerous thing to destroy a system, especially when you have nothing adequate with which to replace it. A whole generation of young Christians saw the system by which their parents and grandparents and great-grandparents had met and married dismantled in front of their eyes. And nothing helpful or useful was set up in its place, only a bunch of difficult, even overwhelming rules that, as Olasky says, induce "both paralysis and pressure." Marriage was elevated to an immensely high pedestal, while at the same time the conditions for getting there were made almost impossible.

◆ ◆ ◆

Do you begin to see why I said the church has a lot to answer for in this area? I believe there were thousands of kindly, well-meaning Christians out there who thought the courtship system was just a slightly holier way of getting the kids where they were bound to end up anyway: married with children. They thought that everything would proceed pretty much as it always had. They didn't see what they were really doing.

They didn't see the confusion and frustration of young adults who were taught that their every romantic impulse should be stifled and suffocated, while they sat around waiting for some sort of big neon sign to descend from heaven and point out their God-chosen mate. They didn't see the relentless pressure that these young adults came under to conform to the courtship system. (To give just one example from my own memory, there was an editor at a very popular Christian website for young adults who used to hammer away relentlessly at any commenter who dared to question what he called "biblical dating"—another name for courtship—claiming that they were attacking the very Bible itself.)

They didn't know what they were creating: a population of young men and women for whom romance and marriage were so difficult to achieve, the very idea of those things so warped and distorted, that many finally just gave up and resigned themselves to lifelong singleness.

Or, even worse, went a step further and turned against each other.

• • •

EIGHT

FRIENDLY FIRE

A single guy—I'll call him Andrew—recently posted in a Christian Facebook group to which I belong. He was spending yet another evening alone, he wrote, watching old screwball comedies.

Part of the trouble with his love life, he speculated, was that Christians are put off by people's flaws, that they're "looking for perfection," and that Christian women in particular are too judgmental, ignoring their own flaws (such as daddy issues and the desire for lots of money) while picking at flaws in others. One or two other guys in the group agreed with him.

On a whim, I decided to try something. Here's what I wrote.

> I'm a devout, churchgoing, celibate Christian woman. I don't expect lots of money or a high-powered job. I don't expect perfection (not being perfect myself). I don't expect movie-star looks, although basic hygiene would be nice. I would

like to find a kind, humble, loyal Christian man with a good sense of humor. I'm a little shy and reserved in person but will warm up to a nice person who treats me with consideration and patience, and I've been told that I'm funny and good company. I don't have daddy issues, as my dad is a thoroughly good egg. I would like to have kids (biological or adopted, whichever works out) and we'll need to be able to support them, but I'm happy to contribute my earnings to the project. And as long as we can feed and clothe and educate them, we don't have to give them swimming pools and polo ponies.

Oh, and I love black-and-white screwball comedies.

So who wants to ask me out?

I wrote this for a few reasons. One was just to vent my frustrations (hopefully, in a creative and joking way) about having heard too many times from Christian men about the impossible standards of Christian women. Another was to help encourage Andrew to stop generalizing about an entire sex and start thinking of us in terms of individuals—always an important and valuable exercise, I believe. Still another was to help remind him of something that's true of most (if not all) of us singles: we all have standards and preferences. Which should make us stop and think before criticizing other people for having them.

To his credit, Andrew quickly realized this. (Also, he was a good sport about letting me write about this conversation here.) "I would love to ask you out," he wrote, "but I live [across the country]." So proximity was a standard. "But I do not want kids." Another standard, and a very significant one. His own preferences were playing a role here too—as I pointed out to him, although he had a right not to want kids, many women do want them and would take that into account when trying to find a spouse. And that could hardly be called a bad or unreasonable desire.

Besides this, Andrew came to realize that the feelings he was projecting onto women were based on some major misconceptions, and possibly also stemming in part from his feelings about himself:

> I was literally just writing a long post about how "Christian women want this perfect man, and I can never be that!" I was literally writing the word[s] "Prince Charming" just before I noticed this thread. I think I'm cutting myself down at the knees because I believe women want something that I can't provide.[1]

That conversation ended up going in a positive and helpful direction, in large part because listening took place and generalizations were eschewed. I wish—how I wish—that more such conversations on these topics would do likewise. Instead, I often find myself reeling away from them feeling bruised and bloodied. Discussions among Christian singles, especially mixed-gender discussions, often have a tendency to turn into hotbeds of blame, resentment, and toxic hostility.

It is so fatally easy, when we're hurting or unhappy or even just discontented, to look around for someone to blame.[2] Perhaps it's all the easier when we've already had so much blame thrown at us that we feel constantly put on the defensive, wanting to strike back at something or someone. With single people, this often translates into blaming the opposite sex as a whole—and that can lead us to some very bad places.

Why do I bring this up here? Because I think this is another area where the church has unwittingly helped cause some misconceptions that have led to difficulties for single people—and also because I believe the church is uniquely equipped to help clear up those misconceptions.

The Blame Game

Spend some time looking through Christian books, articles, and sermons on relationships between the sexes, both for children and for adults. Some clear patterns begin to take shape:

- Women are princesses; men are knights. You may remember that I mentioned this idea back in the introduction to this book.
- Men must lead; women must follow. This is sometimes said to apply not just to the marriage relationship but to all male-female relationships, including dating relationships and even business relationships. For instance, Pastor John Piper, of the popular Desiring God ministry, has argued, "To the degree that a woman's influence over a man, guidance of a man, leadership of a man, is personal and a directive, it will generally offend a man's good, God-given sense of responsibility and leadership, and thus controvert God's created order." Thus, Piper went on to say, a godly woman could be a civil engineer but not a drill sergeant, because the latter would give her too much direct and personal authority over men.[3]
- If women are single, they must not be feminine enough. If men are single, they just need to "man up." Either way, the single person's singleness is most likely his or her own fault.

In short, we have been weighed down by a set of expectations and standards that Sir Lancelot himself would have a hard time living up to.

Writer and speaker Bianca Olthoff unwittingly ended up illustrating the catch-22 we've ended up having to deal with. In a blog post about some interviews she'd conducted with single men, she wrote:

> An interesting item to note is that though each man admitted to failing in pursuing women they were interested in, **every one said they would want to do the pursuing.** *I'm not an archaic meat-head*—joked John—*but there is something thrilling about chasing a girl and having her reciprocate the feelings. If she's too forward, it comes off as desperate. FYI ladies, we can all hear your biological clock.*[4]

You see the problem, right? These men are saying that they want to pursue but they won't pursue—but they don't want the women to pursue, either. Stymied. (FYI John, we can all hear your indecision!)

The result of all this is twofold: single Christians start feeling bad about themselves. And they also start getting angry at each other.

Think about it. If you're a single Christian man who is having a lot of trouble finding the right woman, it's so tempting to go along with all those church leaders who tell you that Christian women have become too independent and too self-centered to appreciate a good man. Similarly, if you're a single Christian woman who hasn't had a date in a while, it's really easy to start believing the ones who tell you that Christian men have become too soft, lazy, and whiny to go out and find a good woman. Either way, you have a nice, neat explanation for the state of things, complete with someone to blame for derailing your life plan: the gender that isn't your own.

But real answers, and real life, are rarely that simple. They don't come wrapped up in neat little packages. And in real life, when you pick a group to scapegoat for your own troubles, it tends to be damaging to your own spiritual and emotional health and your own sense of morality.

It's His Fault

We hear a good deal from evangelical leaders about how hardcore feminists have scapegoated men in this way for years, treating them as either oppressive or useless. This is undeniably a problem. As far as feminism is concerned, I know Christian women who are all over the map—some embrace the term, some shun it, and others carve out a niche for themselves somewhere in between. Even many of those who resist using the term to describe their views will point out that, historically, feminism has done some good, paving the way for women to have the full rights of citizenship, to support themselves, and to make useful contributions to their societies, their families, and their churches.

But the very reason the term causes so much turmoil is that it has long since ceased to be all about equality and has developed destructive, even punitive, aspects. When a professing Christian such as author Dianna E. Anderson claims, "Evangelicalism seems to have encoded rape into its very theology,"[5] or when many Christians claim that a traditionalist interpretation of 1 Timothy 2:11–15 is nothing more than flat-out sexism without even trying to understand the reasons for that centuries-old interpretation,[6] or when single men so often hear themselves described as lazy louts obsessed with video games who refuse to man up, then it is hard to ignore the fact that there is some serious scapegoating going on. And many men, understandably, resent that. They often feel they're being blamed for societal forces beyond their control and that none of their efforts to serve God and behave decently are respected or noticed. Instead, they feel pressured and unappreciated at the same time.

My friend Michelle turns to a favorite movie to describe what she sees going on here:

> *I have this thesis . . . that we're living in Pottersville, because that's what it feels like—the part of* It's a Wonderful Life *where we view the world without George Bailey, the manly man who was willing to make hard sacrifices for those around him, and especially for women. . . . The more I look around, the more I see my friends either a) compromise their beliefs and date/live with/marry non-Christian guys or b) remain single throughout their thirties, despite their attractiveness and sweet hearts. It's a shame, and I honestly think Satan has robbed us of good men—of George Baileys—for many reasons, feminism and the gender-neutral society among them.*

In other words, the push both inside and outside the church to downplay differences between the sexes has left many men, including many Christian men, feeling unsure of their role and their place. This leaves them disinclined to step up and become the kind of man who cares for and works for a family, a home, and a community.

It's Her Fault

Christian writer David Zahl has a long and fascinating article on this trend, titled "Are You Man Enough? When Virile Was a Compliment," which is worth reading in full. Zahl notes a "widespread ambivalence among my peers" about the very idea of masculinity or virility, and quotes a number of other authors who have noticed the same thing. Many men, he observes, hope for daughters instead of sons now because they have no idea how to teach masculine ideals to a son.

> Acceptable masculinity appears to have narrowed just as acceptable femininity has expanded (which . . . says nothing about the validity of those ideals—or their severity). . . . Thus, the amplified apathy and anger we see among today's young men may just be pronounced expressions of the flight and fight responses to the law [the masculine "norm"]. Appeasement as a strategy has largely been abandoned, which translates in many cases to simmering despondency.[7]

Writing in the *Washington Post*, Danielle Paquette adds:

> Some young men, unable to meet the tough-guy stereotype, become ashamed of themselves and start to resent others. Others simply don't want to embody that stereotype but feel pressure to perform it. The economic circumstances of young men might complicate these narratives, in expected and unexpected ways.[8]

For some time now, this unmoored feeling among men has been stirring up a backlash that the church isn't always aware of and so fails to address, though it's affecting many of us in ways large and small. Now it's not just that women are falling for hardcore feminism; many single Christian men in recent years have become easy targets for Men's Rights Activists (MRAs) and members of the Men Going Their Own Way (MGTOW) movement. Show me a Christian website targeted at single people or young adults in general, or even just a post on a Christian blog talking about singleness, and I'll show you an MRA or MGTOW, or two or three, in the comments section. These are men who deal in what's often called "toxic masculinity," who believe that men have gotten a raw deal in life and deserve to take it out on women.

What's especially interesting—and ironic—is that, at the heart of the masculine ideal Zahl and Paquette wrote about, is a balance of strength and gentleness. The restraint that is supposed to keep masculine power in check is just as important to this ideal as the power itself. But it seems that the contemporary redefining, or undefining, of gender doesn't actually remove the traditional ideas—it only turns them into a caricature of themselves. "Masculinity is tricky for guys," one twenty-two-year-old man told Paquette. "You want to [be] respectful and a gentleman but that somehow gets seen as nice-guy and pushover. Finding the balance of being an alpha male gorilla and a decent human is sometimes hard since everyone wants to label us as one thing."[9]

So some guys just give up the balancing act altogether and opt for the gorilla. For instance, hardcore MGTOWs and MRAs promote such delightful practices as having sex with and then dumping as many women as possible, but for obvious reasons they tend to tone down that part of the rhetoric when they talk to Christians and just keep the hatred, resentment, and bitterness (I guess because these are somehow supposed to fit better with Christianity than having sex?).

The typical MRA or MGTOW rant includes a statistic, or two or three, about divorce, usually involving the percentage of women who initiate divorces and/or the percentage of mothers who get custody. It then goes on to draw the conclusion that the marital deck is stacked against men before they ever even propose. And it winds up warning men to stay away from marriage altogether, since it's a losing game. (There also tends to be a lot of bloviating about alpha males and beta males, which is largely irrelevant here but useful for confirming that what you're looking at comes from an MRA or MGTOW.)

It's absolutely crucial here to separate out the facts from the emotions (especially since this is the very thing these movements rely on people *not* doing). As Joylon Jenkins reports in a *BBC Radio 4* segment on the phenomenon, "They'd like you to think they've arrived at their politics through the exercise of pure reason, but at the roots there's usually some private, personal hurt."[10]

It's certainly worth talking about whether divorce law is unfair to men and, if so, what should be done about it. I think most of us could agree on that. However, it's *not* worth encouraging all men to do all they can to punish all women for the state of things. But this is what these men do. Too many Christian men fall for the idea, and too many Christian women end up suffering for it. This view has leached into mainstream Christianity to an extent we don't always realize. Here, for instance, is popular Christian conservative writer Suzanne Venker in an article titled "Why Men Won't Marry You" that went viral:

> What exactly does marriage offer men today? "Men know
> there's a good chance they'll lose their friends, their respect,

their space, their sex life, their money and—if it all goes wrong—their family," says Helen Smith, PhD, author of "Men on Strike." "They don't want to enter into a legal contract with someone who could effectively take half their savings, pension and property when the honeymoon period is over. Men aren't wimping out by staying unmarried or being commitment phobes. They're being smart."

Unlike women, men lose all power after they say "I do." Their masculinity dies, too.[11]

Do you see what's happened here? We've done absolutely nothing to rectify the problems men are facing; we've merely flipped things around so that now *women* are being blamed for societal forces beyond their control. Venker, and Smith as well, simply take for granted that women are out to get men and that the deck is stacked against men even if their prospective wives don't take them for everything they have. They make it sound as if women are inherently bad for men and that's just the way things are.

Analysts like Venker claim to be champions of men, dedicated to making conditions fairer and more just for them. Instead, they're just stirring the pot to no purpose, making things worse for both men and women. Can you imagine how hurtful it is for a single woman to check her Facebook feed and see friend after friend (usually married friends) enthusiastically sharing an article called "Why Men Won't Marry You"—with the added barb that many of the reasons given in the article are things she didn't cause and can't do anything about? (The divorce revolution took place long before most of us now on the singles scene got there!) The views that have infiltrated the pro-marriage movement are rapidly turning it into an anti-marriage movement.

✦ ✦ ✦

Let me offer one small example of how all this played out recently for me. Sociologist W. Bradford Wilcox, whom I mentioned back in section 1, wrote an article called "The Divorce Revolution Has Bred an Army of Woman Haters" for the *Federalist*. Wilcox wrote of an "outpouring of rage, pain, and despair" that he saw in response to a video he'd made about how marriage benefits men. The men he was hearing from didn't believe that contention for a red-hot second.

Wilcox wrote:

Lots of men out there harbor a deeply misogynistic view of the opposite sex, an unremittingly negative view of love and commitment, and a complete lack of faith in marriage to deliver on their deepest dreams and desires . . . a lot of this negativity toward marriage is about divorce.[12]

Wilcox went on to list many of the ways that divorce has hurt men, including financial damage and lost time with their kids, and concluded:

It's this experience of divorce, or the expectation of divorce, that leaves many men reluctant to tie the knot. In Craig's words [one of the men who had responded to Wilcox's video], "I'm currently dating an attractive girl who treats me very well compared to my friends' girlfriends but I would never get married . . . nor will I ever have kids with any woman unless guaranteed 50-50 custody with no child support was made into [family] law as it should be." Needless to say, given the character of family law today, Craig is unlikely to be heading to the altar anytime soon.[13]

As I've made clear, Wilcox was hardly the first person to write about these trends. But he was unusual in (1) keeping the blame fixed on the divorce revolution itself instead of finding a way to blame it on women and (2) calling misogyny what it is and not justifying it.

I tweeted my thanks to Wilcox for his article, mentioning that the phenomenon he described is tough on single women who've never been married or divorced but come in for plenty of anger anyway, just for being women and being out there looking for a nice man to settle down with. In response, another man tweeted to me, "What is the incentive for a man to take that risk?"

I knew from experience that there was absolutely no way for me to answer this question. If he was asking a hypothetical question about what marriage to me would offer, I could have told my questioner that I think I would make a good wife and mother and that I'm no more a fan of divorce than he is—that I believe that, short of abuse or adultery, couples should make every effort to stay together and work their problems out. But that's not what he was looking for. Note the language of "risk" he used—he was looking for an ironclad guarantee that everything would work out well for him. But if I had picked up on this and suggested that there are no guarantees, that everything in life is a risk, then I really would have let myself in for it. We would have been sucked into an endless spiral of arguing, with him out to prove that men are expected to risk too much in today's world and that marriage is a case of all risk and no reward—and not willing to listen to any of my counterarguments. We probably would have ended up with him declaring, just like the man in Wilcox's article, that he would never marry unless the divorce laws change, and since I have no power to change them, he'd be uninterested in anything further I had to say. I'm not trying to be harsh or unfair. I've simply seen too often how this sort of thing goes, and I know what the underlying sentiment is: an utter refusal to believe that women and marriage have anything to recommend them. So I said nothing at all. There was nothing I could say.

Sanctified Blame

But why do Christian men in particular get sucked into this way of thinking? What might make some of them buy into the idea that no woman, no marriage, could possibly be worth it, that all women are out to get them—and that the only good purpose for women is to be used, dumped, and silenced? And what might allow people who believe such things, even to a limited extent, to make inroads into the mainstream church?

Good question. Could it perhaps have something to do with widespread evangelical support of leaders and thinkers like Mark Driscoll, who has notoriously slammed unmarried men (saying they "cannot fully reflect God"[14]), written about women as if they were less than human and about marriage as if it existed solely for the fulfillment of men's sexual needs,[15] and used the adjective "chickified" as a synonym for "bad and weak"?[16] As the *New Republic* points out:

> In content and delivery, Driscoll's ministry mirrored facets of the "pick-up artist" movement, a self-improvement industry generated, according to Katie J. M. Baker, out of "neuro-linguistic programming 'speed seduction' theories in the early 1990s," which promises to get frustrated men into

bed with the women of their dreams. With books like Neil Strauss' 2005 *The Game: Penetrating the Secret Society of Pickup Artists* and Erik Von Markovik's 2007 *The Mystery Method: How to Get Beautiful Women into Bed* forming its core narratives, the PUA world now convenes largely online, in designated forums and discussion boards.

Its books, talks, seminars and videos all presuppose those seeking its wisdom are losers of one sort or another, though the source of male short-coming is often chalked up to institutionalized anti-masculinity in homes, schools, and society at large. There is as much disdain for women as desire for them, and the techniques developed by PUAs tend to focus on fulfilling both urges at once.[17]

And the "pick-up artist" movement is a subset of guess what larger movement? You nailed it.

To put it as mildly as possible, this sort of rhetoric is not an incitement to holiness. It's a spur toward divisiveness and anger. It takes that resentment so many men feel against the scapegoating they've undergone and weaponizes it. It turns the scapegoating in the other direction and escalates the conflict. And it helps to shape men and women who are easy prey for the very un-Christian forces in the world that feed on and encourage anger and hatred. When you consider that we are supposed to be followers of the One who said, "By this all will know that you are My disciples, if you have love for one another,"[18] the sheer scope and nature of the disconnect boggle the mind.

Even leaders far less controversial than Driscoll have fallen into similar, if somewhat tamer, habits, using rhetoric that can breed resentment, encourage blameshifting, and basically urge each sex to think badly of the other. As we've seen, even widely respected and beloved pastors such as Al Mohler and John Piper are not immune to the tendency to say things that can pit various groups (single vs. married, men vs. women) against each other. To borrow from the philosopher David Hume, they confuse an "is" with an "ought to be." In other words, they see the situation that exists—frustration and bitterness among single people—and they seem to believe, consciously or not, that things are this way for a good reason—singleness *should* lead to frustration and bitterness, because marriage is the superior state and anyone who doesn't achieve it *ought* to have bad feelings as a result.

Thus, it seems, it's perfectly justifiable to stimulate these feelings among the single people in hopes of spurring them toward matrimony. If only everyone would just shape up and get married, all the bad feelings would go away and everything would get better.

But that's not what Scripture teaches us, is it?

On the contrary, God's Word suggests rather strongly that when you've made a habit of indulging your own bad feelings, or encouraging someone else's, they're not so easy to turn off. "But each one is tempted when he is drawn away by his own desires and enticed. Then, when desire has conceived, it gives birth to sin; and sin, when it is full-grown, brings forth death" (James 1:14–15).

On the other hand, Paul shows us in his letter to the Romans what a more positive progression can look like: "We also glory in tribulations, knowing that tribulation produces perseverance; and perseverance, character; and character, hope. Now hope does not disappoint, because the love of God has been poured out in our hearts by the Holy Spirit who was given to us" (Rom. 5:3–5). If we are taught to let

God work through our tribulations to produce these good qualities in us, we can learn to live godly lives without bitterness, whether married or single—and, it need hardly be said, those of us who do get married will have learned habits that will help create strong and healthy marriages. Surely that's a better idea than provoking resentment between the sexes over what we're all supposedly owed.

But bad teachings die hard. Some of my interviewees told me about messages they'd heard in church in recent years that were quite definite about what the sexes were "owed" and how they were supposed to behave.

I had a negative experience in one church setting in which it was emphasized just how little the men [in the church] regarded the women of our family (to the extent that in an argument, they would not even speak to us women directly with any concerns but rather talk to the man of the household).—Charity

[I was taught] that men were to be strong in all areas of life and that women were to be strong in some areas of life.—Veronica

[When I was growing up] married men were often authoritarian and their view of women's roles was to stay silent in church and simply have and raise babies and care for their needs.—Fiona

[I was taught] that a woman's only place is in marriage and being at home.—Scott

If that were true—if all women were meant to be in the home, carrying out the duties of homemaker and thinking of nothing else, and if too many of them were refusing to live out that destiny—then yes, perhaps men would have a right to be angry. Conversely, if all men were meant to fit into the mold of big strong tough guy, invincible and impervious to pain, capable of protecting and providing all things for his family without breaking a sweat, but they were increasingly refusing to jump on the white horse and fulfill that mission, then perhaps women would have a right to be angry.

But again, that's not what Scripture teaches us. It doesn't teach us that the different genders owe each other anything— or have a right to expect each other to fit the perfect culturally created mold. And it certainly doesn't teach that resentment and anger are righteous responses to the failure of our expectations or that getting married automatically cures us of these bad habits. (On this subject of what we're "owed," I once witnessed an amusing Facebook conversation between two guys, one of whom was lamenting that the woman he deserved had not yet shown up in his life. Guy #2 gently pointed out that as a devout Calvinist, guy #1 was not supposed to believe that he deserved anything good at all. Guy #1 was suddenly a very sheepish Calvinist indeed.)

❖ ❖ ❖

The entitlement mentality and the tendency to scapegoat seem to have rooted themselves deep within the church, often coming directly from those we trust to lead and guide us spiritually. But those who get dragged into these clashes, or even those who just find themselves dealing with the fallout, can testify that—as you might expect from unbiblical teachings and practices—they are deeply hurtful to the body of Christ.

For example, how many times have you heard people—both men and women—say that the church has been feminized . . . and how often do they mean it in a good way? The evangelical church has slipped into the habit of using a word that refers to women as a word that means all things sentimental, sloppy, and generally non-appealing—even though, truth be told, many women hate those things just as much as men do.

Similarly, how often have you heard single women described as "too strong" to get married, or heard Christians deride single men as the sort of guys who live in their mother's basement and play video games all day, or heard people in the church speculating on the sexuality of those who have remained single? Much of the time, those descriptions have nothing to do with the actual people we're talking about and everything to do with stereotypes based on faulty thinking. We've got some pervasive mental images of single people that have made their way through the church like a virus, the sort of thing that's very easy to catch before you even knew it was in the air.

With so many within the church pushing harmful attitudes like these, communication between the sexes increasingly breaks down. Many Christian single women are afraid even to express an opinion for fear they'll be seen as too bold, too forward, too high-maintenance, and various other things that the Victorians would have disliked.

I myself, as you've no doubt gathered by now, am *not* afraid to express an opinion. Yet even I get affected by the atmosphere and the weird, outdated expectations that surround so many male-female interactions in today's evangelical church. Sometimes I watch TV or movies and I honestly can't help but feel astonished to see female characters who sass their men and don't get penalized—in fact, whose sass brings the men back wanting more. Even (or perhaps especially) in movies of the 1930s, '40s, and '50s, for which I have a passion, women like Rosalind Russell and Bette Davis seem to get away with a lot more than many modern churchgoing women. I'm not saying that Hollywood is always known for portraying realistic or desirable relationships, but I don't think the entertainment industry is exaggerating all *that* much when it suggests there are some men who can handle, even enjoy, women speaking their minds.

It makes me feel more than a little wistful when I come back to earth and look again at the Christian singles scene. Everyone always warns us women about getting swept away by glamorous movie romances starring dashing leading men, and setting our expectations far too high based on the fantasies onscreen. No one tells us that we might get even more swept away by the prospect of a romance in which a woman can simply share her thoughts and feelings without causing the man to sprint for the exit.

Everything I've been describing here, I believe, results from holding people to standards that are unrealistic and unbiblical. We as a church seem to have decided that the Bible's balanced treatment of marriage and singleness, of men and women, is not good enough. We wanted something better, holier, higher.

But as we should have known would happen all along—because it always happens when people think they know better than God—in trying to create something better than what God offered us, we've instead managed to create an unholy mess.

◆ ◆ ◆

TWO STORIES

Sometimes when I'm thinking about Christian views and expectations about romance and gender, I think about two different book series by Christian writers I encountered when I was younger that frame the issues in very different ways. I bring them up here because I think one of them encapsulates many contemporary church teachings on gender and relationships and the expectations that go with those—and the other offers a model for how those teachings could be better.

Christy and Todd

The Christy Miller series by Robin Jones Gunn was very popular among Christian teenagers when I was growing up—and it's still fairly popular, judging by its Amazon rankings and Goodreads reviews. I was a bit young for the books when they first started coming out in the late '80s, but my older sister had a few of them, and I used to swipe them to read when she wasn't around.

Christy Miller is a character whom many teen girls can relate to: awkward, insecure, longing for popularity and prettiness and all the things that other girls seem to have. Christy's love interest is Todd Spencer, who is a gorgeous blond surfer with "screaming silver-blue eyes" (because of course he is) whom she met on a beach vacation with her uncle and aunt. After he helps lead her to Christ in the first book, *Summer Promise*, they start an on-again, off-again friendship-romance sort of thing that goes on for multiple books—just friendshippy enough to fall in line with Christian courtship culture, just romantic enough to keep teens reading.

The plotlines of these novels usually follow one of two patterns: (1) Todd hasn't been around for a while, and Christy feels distant from him and finds it hard to trust God, or (2) Todd is around but acting all quiet and mysterious, and Christy feels distant from him and finds it hard to trust God. Then Todd (1) reappears or (2) explains himself, and all is right with the world and Christy realizes she should never stop trusting God and Todd.

I group those two together for a reason: Todd is Christy's model of all that is godly. His dialogue consists mostly of quoting the Bible, praising Christy for dressing modestly or not coming on to him too strongly, and telling her that he wants to be her friend but maybe someday more than her friend but right now just her friend—but her really *really* special friend who kisses her in the middle of the street and gives her a bracelet that reads "Forever." Which means he wants to be her *friend* forever. All clear?

And Todd's periods of silence and distance usually just mean he's busy doing something saintly that makes Christy feel small if she doesn't like it—like the time he informs her that he's asked a schoolmate in a wheelchair to the prom instead of her, without having checked with Christy first to see if she was okay with it. ("I knew you'd understand and everything, but, I don't know . . . I guess sometimes girls get their feelings hurt over nothing."[1]) And this is after he's pontificated about how the prom is inferior and unworthy anyway because it's nothing like the Marriage Supper of the Lamb will be in heaven.

Small surprise that in his prom pictures, Todd "looked finer than any"—wait for it—"knight in shining armor."[2]

Christy's conversation with another character about Todd from book 6, *A Heart Full of Hope*, pretty much sums it up:

> "What is it about him? Why is he still so important to you? Did he write you love poems or make big promises about your future?"
>
> Christy couldn't help but laugh. "No. Todd has never written me a letter or note of any kind. And he is about the most non-committal person I've ever known."
>
> "Then what's the deal with him? What makes you so drawn to him?"
>
> Christy had to think about it. Rick was right; some kind of bond existed between her and Todd. How could she explain it?
>
> "I think it's the Lord," Christy said finally. "I think what makes Todd unique is that he prays with me and—" . . .
>
> In trying to find the words to explain Todd's uniqueness, she remembered how Todd would look when he talked about God. It was a contented, vulnerable, strong-as-a-rock look. That was it. Todd loved Jesus more than anything.[3]

On the surface, all this may sound great, but even as a teenager I sensed something a little off about the distant and holy Todd, and about the whole relationship. I do give Robin Jones Gunn credit for this much: she was trying to show girls that conventional romance may not be all it's cracked up to be, that countercultural ways of doing things can work in a sex-obsessed world, and that a genuinely good guy is worth waiting for. Those are laudable goals, and to some extent Gunn succeeded in meeting them.

But I think she erred in making Todd's faith his only distinguishing characteristic, apart from good looks (if these were the only things that drew Christy to him, what stopped her from falling in love with any other good-looking, devout Christian young man?), in trying to make something grand and spiritual out of what really just sounds like flakiness (only in a Christian teen romance novel would "noncommittal" be seen as a good quality in a guy), and in generally making their relationship too much like that of a saint on a pedestal and his adoring young disciple. Things are out of balance here. Though Christy at least has a personality, it doesn't feel like she's genuinely Todd's equal.

That was one of my earliest experiences with a Christian author's depiction of romance. In college, I would have a very different one.

Harriet and Peter

In a class on "Theology and Oxford Christian Writers," I was assigned to read Dorothy L. Sayers's mystery novel *Gaudy Night*, and I was so taken with it that I immediately went on to read the rest of her Lord Peter Wimsey series,

written in the 1920s and '30s. Interestingly, although Sayers
was a devout Christian (and a good friend of C. S. Lewis
and Charles Williams), she wasn't writing about Christian
characters. Peter Wimsey and Harriet Vane are flawed human
beings; they've made serious mistakes and suffered some very
serious consequences. And they certainly don't live inside a
safe and pretty bubble. But through bitter experience, each
of them has learned some important things about life and
relationships.

Sayers did make her amateur sleuth something of a super-
hero, often to comic effect: he is super-rich, super-smart, and
super-talented. (Fortunately, she refrained from making him
tall and handsome, or he might have turned out completely
insufferable. No silver-blue eyes, screaming or otherwise,
for his lordship.) But interestingly, when it came to romance,
she dropped the super-heroics and went in for realism; she
gives us a sometimes stormy but always honest relationship
between two intelligent, well-rounded adults.

Though her books aren't explicitly Christian, elements
of Sayers's Christian worldview leak through, particularly
in the way her characters treat each other. Peter gently helps
Harriet regain her confidence after a previous romance gone
very bad, but not by being a savior figure—only by consistently showing how much he respects and values her. "If you
have found your own value," he tells her in the book *Gaudy
Night*, when they're looking back at the progress of their
relationship, with all its misunderstandings and missteps,
"that is immeasurably the greatest thing."[4]

Peter also shows respect for Harriet and belief in her worth
by talking with her like a rational person, instead of, say, blurt-
ing out Bible verses and random spiritual musings and leaving

her to try to decipher his meaning. Harriet, for her part, starts out suspicious and afraid to trust but gradually learns to see and appreciate Peter's good qualities and to care deeply for him. Maybe it's a little unfair to compare these two series. One was written specifically for (and about) teenagers and the other for a general adult audience; one was intended to follow a specific Christian formula, and the other is simply part of the mystery genre; one was written to teach and the other to entertain. The funny thing is, though, I learned a lot more about healthy views of gender and relationships from the mainstream "entertainment" series.

Just the idea that book characters in love (or on the way there) were actually able to go through life having down-to-earth conversations about everyday topics was something of an eye-opener. So was the idea that it might be a good idea to try to live fully in the time one is born in, rather than letting all one's ideas and values be shaped by a kind of vague and wistful nostalgia. The fact that a Christian was suggesting these things, so at odds with so much of what we hear from the church today, made a deep impression on me.

There's a scene in one of Sayers's novels, *Have His Carcase* (first published in 1936), where Harriet walks into a hotel lounge while a dance is going on. Many of the people there are dressed in Victorian-style formal wear, which was apparently experiencing a resurgence in popularity during this particular period.

"But it was so obviously an imitation," Harriet notes. Not just the style of dress but "the sidelong glances, the downcast eyes, the mock-modesty of the women." Are the men on this dance floor, she wonders, foolish enough to believe that old-fashioned attitudes have experienced a comeback along with old-fashioned outfits? "'Hardly,' thought Harriet, 'when they know perfectly well that one has only to remove the train and the bustle, get into a short skirt and walk off, with a job to do and money in one's pocket. Oh, well, it's a game, and presumably they all know the rules.'"[5]

As a matter of fact, though, not all of the people Harriet sees at the dance do know the rules—and in the course of the story, some will be deeply hurt because of it. It turns out that games can be dangerous.

No More Games

Because of all the "You are God's princess," "Jesus is all you need" messages that often come across in mating, dating, and relating books, it leaves a lot of disillusioned women waiting for princes without a lot of practical advice on where to find them or how to make yourself available.—Ashley

So much of the knights-and-princesses stuff going on in the church these days seems like a game—but again, not many people seem to know the rules. Perhaps it's time we faced facts: knights and princesses can be a lot of fun to read about in fairytales, but for all intents and purposes, they're completely outmoded in real-life twenty-first-century America. None of it has any bearing on the world we live in now, and it does little good—and much harm—to pretend otherwise, to single people or to anyone else. It distorts reality, inflates expectations beyond all reason, and too often ends in disillusionment and bitterness. What's frequently sold to us as wholesome ideas about romance, both in fiction and in nonfiction, is full of ideas that undermine both our self-worth and our understanding of relationships.

However your church interprets Ephesians 5, the much-disputed passage about male headship in marriage, I can't see how any reasonable interpretation leads either to men being godlike (or Todd-like) spiritual gurus and women being their humble acolytes or to women being pristine objects of desire and men groveling at their feet. When it loads us down with these unbiblical and unrealistic ideas, the church gives to single people of both sexes burdens too heavy to bear. And for those who do eventually achieve marriage, it gives them a shaky foundation to build on.

We single Christians don't need fairytales, and we don't need hoops to jump through or obstacle courses to conquer. We need to hear truly godly, practical wisdom on how to trust, how to respect, how to forgive, how to be patient and kind—all the things that go into creating and sustaining strong relationships with the opposite sex. We need to be reminded that Christ calls us, with His help, to approach each other with love and understanding, not to barricade ourselves behind walls formed by pain and pride. We need to be taught how to really listen to people and appreciate who they are, not just make assumptions about them and then blame them for those assumptions.

In short, we single Christians need the church to stop teaching us to play games and start teaching us to live in the real world. In order to do that, I would suggest, there are quite a few concepts and traditions—cherished yet ultimately unbiblical concepts and traditions that "[make] the word of God of no effect"[6]—that the church as a whole needs to start rethinking.

Where Do We Go from Here?

TEN

◆ ◆ ◆

RETHINKING OUR VALUES

Your daughters might not have a home to make in the traditional sense that we revere and that so many women strive for. This is a problem only if this ideal becomes idolized. We are individuals, thumb-printed by God, whose design differs from person to person; we are not called each and all to the same earthly end.

Rachel McMillan[1]

As I was working on this book, a much-publicized article came out in *New York* magazine, hailing the rise of the single female voter. Author Rebecca Traister wrote:

The rise of the single woman is an exciting turn of historical events because it entails a complete rethinking of who women are and what family is and who holds dominion within it—and outside it. . . . Beyond whether you regard this shift as dangerous or thrilling, it is having a profound effect on our politics.[2]

Obviously, this is a thesis with significant implications for Christians, most of whom have deeply held faith-based beliefs on these subjects and on what kind of effect they should have on our politics and on our world in general. That's why Anika Smith, a friend of mine, wrote a thoughtful response. Tackling some of Traister's ideas about how the demographic shift would work and advocating a broader view of the matter, Smith argued:

> Single women need more than the promise of government benefits or tax cuts. They need to know that they are seen, that they contribute to our society, and ultimately, that their lives matter. . . . Above all the policy proposals, single women need to know there is a place for them at the grown-ups' table.[3]

The very first comment left on Smith's piece read, in part:

> The core function of a culture is to propagate its values. The new "single-woman" phenomena is [sic] irrelevant to that core function and is thus just another sociological dysfunction reflective of a culture in the process of going out of business. . . . The political power of single women tends toward a society that is hostile to the masculine nature in either stunting the transformation of males such that they never become men or perverting the transformation of men such that they become oppressors of women and destructive of a society they deem effeminate and offensive.
>
> The new "single woman" will not produce children in numbers needed to sustain the culture and would not be able to pass on values that can sustain the culture in the face of its multiplying enemies even if she did.[4]

I offer this anecdote to illustrate the practical effect of a Christian culture that goes beyond viewing marriage as the good and important thing that it is and turns it into an idol. A blog comment is only a blog comment and shouldn't be made to carry too much weight, but as any writer will tell you, the comments section often reflects some very widely held views. And we might say that the comment on Anika Smith's article represents the triumph of Morkenism. Remember Dr. Hubert Morken, back in the introduction, the instructor who stated that having babies was the way to win the culture for Christ? This is simply his viewpoint carried to its logical conclusion. If marriage and childbearing is *the* way that you make a difference for Christ, then how can there be any role for those who are not married and not having children?

If people really believe that, then they can't share in the vision Smith was writing about, in which everyone is invited to the table and has something important to offer. All they can do is see some people as successes and some as failures, based on marital and parental status.

At the heart of this problem, I think, is that too many Christians, when they notice writers like Rebecca Traister celebrating singleness, instantly see red flags and hear alarm bells. They fall into the trap of thinking that if a nonbeliever thinks that the rise of single women is a good thing, then it must necessarily be a bad thing. They buy into the cultural and political perceptions of all the Rebecca Traisters out there, who believe that single women's values and priorities must necessarily clash with those of the church. They fail to look at the phenomenon and ask how the church might reach those single women, not to mention how those women might possibly end up blessing and benefiting the church.

In short, they're not approaching the situation from a Christian worldview. They're approaching it from a worldly one—the kind of worldview that looks at a group of people, asks "What can they do for us?" and, failing to find a satisfactory answer, writes them off. Which is completely the opposite of the way Jesus Christ looked at people.

So, even leaving aside the idea that spreading your worldview through outbreeding nonbelievers has more to do with Darwin than with Christ, Morken's school of thought has obvious limitations and flaws. If there truly is room in the body of Christ for the single as well as the married person—and the New Testament makes it very clear that there is—then something about his theory must be off.

But he's not alone. When the evangelical church as a whole slips into a belief in marriage and family as the highest good, as I've been arguing that it has, you're going to find faulty thinking, bad theology, and subpar treatment of singles all over the place.

Let's look at a few key concepts that demonstrate this.

Identity

If someone asked you "Who are you?" and you had to answer without taking time to think about it, what would you say? The chances are good that you would define yourself in one of two ways: through your relationships or through your work.

By and large, the church has been good about teaching us to avoid the latter error, reminding us frequently that we're more than what we do for a living. This is a much-needed reminder (especially for those of us who live in places like the Washington, DC, area, where, according to the secular mindset, what you do for a living is *everything*).

But when it comes to defining ourselves through our relationships . . . that's a different story. This is the kind of error that today's church is all too prone to let us get away with, or even encourage.

And this error creeps into our thinking in the most insidious ways, coloring everything we look at or think about. Here are just a few examples I've seen in recent months:

- A woman's name is dragged into a political scandal, and people protest, "Leave her alone, she's a wife and mother!" And the single, childless woman following all this thinks, *What if she weren't? Would she still be worth defending?*

- An anti-porn speaker asks men to consider the fact that a given woman in a pornographic video is someone's daughter or sister, and some think, *But what if she weren't? Does she have value without any of those relationships?*

- We hear of a man who died in an accident or of a terrible disease, and then we're told that the worst part is that he left a wife and children. *But what if he hadn't? Would that make his suffering and death somehow more acceptable?*

This is an extremely tricky minefield to navigate. For one thing, it's natural to concentrate on how others may be suffering because of their loved one's trauma or absence—most if not all of us have been through such suffering before and can easily relate to it and sympathize with it in others. And it's especially hard to think of children suffering such a permanent and traumatic loss. For another thing, because our relationships are so vital and valuable, so integral to our lives, we can hardly think of ourselves or others apart from them.

And that is not a bad thing in itself. It's our very nature to live in relationship to one another and to God; it's how we were created. So as I've stressed throughout this book, community matters, especially to Christians. We need it to thrive. And because we're all so familiar with that need, we often end up seeing everyone and everything through that particular lens.

The problem starts when we make the leap, as many of us all too easily do, to believing that our identity lies in those relationships. That's what leads us to place more value on those who have more and better relationships and less on those who haven't had the opportunity to form as many. And as for those who once had them, such as the divorced—well, as Christian divorcée Dena Johnson writes, "It seems as if people everywhere want you to wear a large, scarlet letter 'D' around your neck. . . . You are often scorned by the church because of your past."[5]

All this draws us away from the truth that our real identity is found in God, our Creator and Redeemer. This is the ultimate relationship we were created for, the relationship that is accessible to everyone who places his or her faith in Christ.

This is, at least in part, what pastors mean when they say, "The ground is level at the foot of the cross." Before Christ, the differences that keep us apart fall away. That doesn't mean they don't exist or don't matter but it does mean they don't have to divide us. We can reach past them to accept, support, and love each other. As Paul unforgettably wrote, "There is neither Jew nor Greek, there is neither slave nor free, there is neither male nor female; for you are all one in Christ Jesus" (Gal. 3:28).

If we keep our focus on this truth, we can learn to readjust our thinking. With that readjustment would come some important changes in the way we in the church view each other, and consequently in the way we treat each other. Doubtless it would take some time and there would be bumps along the way, as there are in most worthwhile endeavors.

But with divine guidance and grace, the result could be a truly unified, truly functioning body of Christ—as opposed to a body that's not working right because there are a bunch of leftover parts sitting around that no one knew what to do with. Okay, my metaphor is a little strained, but you get the idea. When we know who a person truly is—a beloved creation of God, bearing His image—other parts of his or her identity are less likely to get in the way of a loving relationship with that person. And that ultimately leads to a church where single people feel welcomed and cared for, not inferior or invisible.

Oddly enough, what comes to mind when I think about how all this might play out on a practical level comes from a book by a secular writer: Chris Bohjalian's bestselling *The Guest Room*. When I explain the story line, you're *really* going to think I'm being odd. But please bear with me. The book is dark and gritty but it's also powerful and insightful. And I think it has a certain relevance here.

Bohjalian tells the story of a bachelor party that spins wildly out of control when a young Russian woman hired as a stripper stabs the guard who was accompanying her. The party's host, Richard, is stricken with guilt over the sordid events that have unfolded in his home—the home where he and his wife are raising their little girl. He feels especially guilty over a moment that happened earlier in the night, when he found himself alone in his own guest room with Alexandra, another of the young strippers at the party. He had almost given in to temptation, almost done the unthinkable, until he felt the goose bumps on her legs and realized "the poor thing was cold."

That moment sparked something in him—a reminder that he was a married man and a father, a realization that "this had all gone too far."[6] And something more: compassion for this girl, barely over legal age, with whom he has nothing at all in common. When he finds out that she was a sex slave, forced into stripping and prostitution against her will, both his guilt and his compassion grow even greater.

Later on, while the two young women are on the run, Richard hears his brother and some of the other party guests recalling the party with enthusiasm despite the brutal turn it took. And it makes him sick.

> She wasn't his daughter—after the party, he could never view her as a daughter—but he had felt a fatherly pang spring from his chest when he had imagined her with his brother or a creep like Spencer. And the idea of her . . . dead? Or hiding? Or hurt? It left him woozy. He recalled that moment when she had taken his arm on the stairs in his home, and there in the restaurant he looked down at the spot near his elbow. She was just a kid. It just wasn't fair.
>
> He felt a wave of sadness nearly smother him and wondered where she was now.[7]

Did you catch that? Richard's heart goes out to this young woman not because of who she's related to, like the anti-porn speaker in my earlier example—somebody's daughter, some-body's sister—but because of who she is: "just a kid." The thought stirs his own fatherly compassion, but he's still not thinking of Alexandra as a daughter—his or anybody else's. He's thinking of her as an individual, a person, with her own troubles and griefs. Eventually, his compassion will lead him to make a great sacrifice to help her—this girl he never saw before and has no real point of connection with—simply because she desperately needs help.[8]

Obviously, Richard is just a character in a book, but he reflects his creator's belief of what an ordinary person, not necessarily a Christian, could be and do. If it's possible that a nonbeliever might be capable of such compassion, how much more should Christians be able to imagine it and put it into practice? What if we in the church saw each other not as people in different categories from us but as fellow human beings with needs—basic needs like comfort, affirmation, and encouragement—we could help fulfill? What would our lives and our churches look like then?

Worth

Closely related to the idea of identity is the idea of worth. Most evangelical Christians will tell you without missing a beat that our worth is found in God and that this makes us all equal in His eyes. But the hidden, unacknowledged, often unrealized hierarchies in many churches tell a different tale.

We've already looked at some of the ways in which churches tend to convey a higher view of married people than single people. These views can be woven so deeply into the fabric of the church that many members never even realize they're there—except, of course, those who feel the brunt of them. This can in turn lead them to question their own worth.

Back in section 1, I referenced the Rev. Al Mohler and his statement that marriage, not work, is "the crucible of our saint-making." I'm bringing this up again because it's a perfect example of what I'm talking about. According to this view, married people have a leg up on the rest of us in the process of becoming saints. Single people have no such crucible. You don't have to go very far, then, to reach the conclusion that single people have less worth.

That thought may never have occurred to Reverend Mohler on a conscious level, and yet somehow, the seeds of it were planted in his thinking. And probably for reasons that have nothing at all to do with theology. Christena Cleveland, a psychologist and professor who writes frequently about faith and singleness, observes: "I can see why the married people (like Dr. Mohler) who run the Church are more inclined to believe that God makes saints exclusively/primarily through marriage. *Research shows that humans intuitively trust people who share their life experiences.*"[9]

According to this view, what Mohler believes about the intrinsic ties between marriage and holiness isn't spiritual at all. It's based on bias—the kind of bias that comes naturally to us all and that often leads us to make mistakes if we're not careful. This is exactly the kind of bias that's rampant in the church, largely because the majority of the church has long consisted of married people.

To put it another way—a way that may be uncomfortable to hear but may also be helpful—married churchgoers in general have developed into a sort of clique. That's become a dirty word in many churches, precisely because so many churchgoers have been hurt by cliques. As Saleama A. Ruvalcaba puts it:

> Church cliques have a huge impact in society as these exclusive groups weaken the kingdom of God. . . . Church cliques are of the world. We watch television and idolize celebrities even though we know nothing about them in real life. We do the same thing in church. People who dress well—a nice-looking couple, a "supermom," the big businessman—we assume are worthy of our praise, so we place a higher value on them than the unassuming person who quietly walks into church looking for love.[10]

If you're not among those Christians who stand in tight little groups gossiping after church and giving the hairy eyeball to any outsider who approaches, then you may think the word *clique* doesn't apply in your case. But that's just a stereotype; the reality can be much more insidious and much harder to spot. If you ever find yourself and your friends slipping into an "us and them" mentality regarding the singles in your church, you may be forming a clique mentality without even realizing it. (Notice I didn't say "us *versus* them." A clique doesn't have to involve enmity or even opposition to be a clique.)

As you know if you've ever been there, the outside of a clique can be a very cold place to be. And as I said before, it can make you start questioning your own worth. If we're all supposed to find our identity in Christ but some Christians experience being shut out in church just because of their marital status, where do we find our refuge, our anchor? Where is there left to go?

And there's more to this whole question of worth than just the experience of being shut out. Tied in with that question is the question of what we deserve out of life. Of course, *deserve* is something of a loaded word to use in a Christian context. As that little anecdote about the two Calvinists reminds us, the official line is that we're all undeserving before God of anything but punishment for our sins, and only His infinite love and grace stand between us and that punishment. But here again, our behavior and our attitudes undermine what we claim to believe. Because Christians often act as if, undeserving though we all may be, the unmarried are *far* less deserving than the married.

I cannot begin to tell you how many times I've seen Christians shaking their heads over the waywardness of singles. I'm not talking now about sexual waywardness or other kinds of hedonistic behavior. I'm talking about behavior like devoting themselves to their jobs, or having pets, or doing other things that supposedly are reserved for married couples to do. These things, we're sometimes told, are a poor substitute for marriage and family, and good single Christians should not be preoccupied with them. (What we *are* supposed to be preoccupied with, I'm not sure. Going through our matches on eHarmony one more time, I guess.)

I believe that most if not all people who say these things mean them sincerely and believe they're saying them for our good. But do you know how it comes across? It makes us feel as if, because we didn't do the proper thing and get married, we don't deserve to enjoy things the way that married people do. We lost life's biggest competition, so we shouldn't get prizes. We messed up; too bad for us.

If that kind of thing doesn't undermine a single person's sense of worth, I don't know what would.

And it gets even worse than that. There are many married Christians who dwell on the idea that the single and childless will one day be old and alone with no one to care for them. *Let them have their fun now*, this narrative goes. *One day they'll be sorry!* I wish I could tell you I was making this up, but I'm not. Making this argument is actually a point of pride with many. They make sure to remind us of our likely future forlorn and abandoned state every chance they get (as if it had never occurred to us).

In short, it sounds like the body of Christ is telling us, "Getting married is your job. If you don't get the job done, don't come crying to us."

But doesn't that look a little different from the biblical ideal? Look at a passage like Acts 4:32–35, for example:

> Now the multitude of those who believed were of one heart and one soul; neither did anyone say that any of the things he possessed was his own, but they had all things in common. And with great power the apostles gave witness to the resurrection of the Lord Jesus. And great grace was upon them all. Nor was there anyone among them who lacked; for all who were possessors of lands or houses sold them, and brought the proceeds of the things that were sold, and laid them at the apostles' feet; and they distributed to each as anyone had need.

Or take James 1:27:

> Pure and undefiled religion before God and the Father is this: to visit orphans and widows in their trouble, and to keep oneself unspotted from the world.

Nowhere in there do we see those without spouses or children punished for their status. Quite the contrary. Their status was seen as an opportunity for others to demonstrate Christian love by caring for them. While Paul could be strict with those who sought support when they didn't really need it (see 1 Tim. 5), their marital or parental status, or lack thereof, was not in itself a target of criticism.

Not only that, but the "don't come crying to us" mentality doesn't take reality into account. Again, it's a sign that we're relying too much on formulas and not taking actual human beings into consideration. And it doesn't even account for those who "did their job" and still ended up alone. Like those whose grown children rebelled and don't speak to them, for whatever reason, or those who have experienced great tragedy and loss.

My father has an elderly friend—they play together in an amateur bluegrass group—who recently had to go to the hospital for a knee operation. He has no family to look after him. His wife is dead and their two children both died young, one in an accident and one from illness. He did everything "right" according to the view I've been describing—he got married, he had a family—and now he's alone. Many of you reading this may have friends or relatives in a similar situation. It happens.

Now, I'm not saying that the modern church never does a good job of caring for its widows and orphans. It very frequently does an excellent job (and I'll get more into this in a later chapter). But to be honest, sometimes the messages the church sends can undermine much of its good work. Once we had a reputation for caring for the lonely and abandoned; now, sadly, we too often make the lonely and abandoned feel they have no place among us. Ironically, sometimes the secular world seems to manage these things better. At the very least, it demonstrates a better understanding of the needs of the lonely and the value of friendship and compassion in meeting those needs.

Not long ago, I was flipping channels one day, looking for something to watch, when I happened on a rerun of the show *How I Met Your Mother*. It's never been one of my regular shows, but the situation unfolding onscreen arrested my attention, and I stopped flipping.

The character Robin had just been told by a doctor that she could never have children, and she was far more taken aback by this news than she expected. Apparently she hadn't wanted children, but as she obliquely remarked to her friends, "It's one thing not to want something. It's another to be told that you can't have it."[11]

Robin couldn't bring herself actually to tell her friends the news—in awkward sitcom fashion, she pretended instead that she had been told she could never be a pole-vaulter—but they knew something was really wrong and made strenuous efforts to cheer her up. Just when she thought she was going to be alone on Christmas, her friend/occasional love interest Ted showed up to spend it with her. And then the narrator, who, according to the premise of the show, was telling all of this as a story to his own children, concluded the episode with this:

> Kids, your Aunt Robin never became a pole-vaulter, but she did become a famous journalist, a successful businesswoman, a world traveler. She was even briefly a bullfighter—that's a funny story, I'll get to that one later. But there's one thing your Aunt Robin never was.[12]

163

I waited for the last sentence: "She was never a mom." But I was wrong. The last sentence was this:

She was never alone.[13]

I almost cried right there in my living room. What a beautiful affirmation of the worth of an individual . . . and how sad that I got it from a TV show instead of from the church of God.

The truth is Robin and the other characters on this show are the kind of people whom the Javerts of the church would say deserve to end up lonely. (You remember Javert from *Les Misérables*? Along with tracking the ex-prisoner Jean Valjean all his life, he was also grumpy about the fact that the prostitute Fantine got to die comfortably in a hospital bed instead of out on the streets.[14]) They, like most standard twenty-first-century sitcom characters, are crude and promiscuous, and several of them are more committed to their careers than to any steady romantic relationship.

And yet somehow, in this case, these godless and hedonistic characters managed to model exactly what Christ taught us to do: demonstrate love—real, deep, affirming, life-changing love—for each other. If TV shows reflect the values of the larger culture, this one was signaling that, for all that our culture gets wrong, it still has a grasp on one thing that's very important.

And it's beginning to look like, if we don't want to be outshone by the world in that department, the church needs to get its act together.

Maturity

I would encourage churches and married Christians to begin to see singles as fully human and fully adult and to acknowledge that even married people often are not fully mature or have "issues" and that marriage is not a reward or prize or graduation to adulthood.—Fiona

As I was doing research and conducting interviews for this book, I noticed that one particular phrase popped up several times. That phrase was "the kids' table." Here's one instance:

It's so easy to build a shiny, attractive children's program, but a singles program is challenging because there is a different dynamic between twenty-five and thirty-five than there is at the thirty-five-plus life stage, and often there's one "college and career" group trying to meet everyone's needs. Singles don't want to feel like they're not allowed at the "big kids' table" because they're not married with children, but that's often what it feels like.—Ashley

Most people have sat at the little kids' table at Thanksgiving or Christmas dinner at some point in their lives. The problem is, many singles feel as if they never get to leave it. Often it seems as if, in the eyes of the married adults around us, we never grew up. We didn't go through the proper steps to maturity, so we haven't reached it. That means we're lumped in with the kids—sometimes literally. (According to the *Seattle Times*, at actual parties and celebrations, "Many hosts don't think twice about sending an unmarried aunt to the kids' table. . . . It's part of a cultural lag from the 1950s."[15])
Writer Lauren Levine puts it this way:

You absolutely want to celebrate your friends' major life milestones with them, so [wedding and baby gift] expenses are okay. But here's the issue: if you haven't found a life partner or decided to have a baby yet, it's like society as a whole doesn't think you count. You're still at the kids' table of life, even if you're doing important and amazing things on your own.[16]

We've already touched on some of the consequences of this mistaken belief within the church. I wrote earlier about churches that send even the older singles off to the young adult ministry. My friend Fiona told me about another consequence that particularly bothers her:

> To a person, my friends with children introduce me and have their children call me Miss First Name. Every other married adult within their circle is Mr. or Mrs. Last Name. Why am I not Miss Last Name? I feel like I'm given a modicum of respect as an elder by the use of a title but then am somehow identified as a little lower than the adults by the use of my first name. . . . I've only felt comfortable enough to ask two friends why they did that, and both responded in several moments of uncomfortable silence before stammering out something along the lines of me being more like an aunt or part of the family, at which point I . . . asked to be addressed as Aunt First Name.

Maybe these seem like little things. But little things add up. Enough of them over time can make a single person feel infantilized and inferior to the "real" grown-ups, the ones who did things properly and hit all the required milestones.

Once again, it's not by accident that singles are made to feel this way, even though few people do it to us intentionally. It's yet another pattern that stems from a worldview deeply ingrained in those around us. Evangelical Christians have a tendency to indulge in nostalgia, sometimes to an unhealthy extent, and one of the things we tend to pine for is the safe, steady, regular succession of milestones in a person's life. With milestones, you know exactly what stage of life a person is in and can treat that person accordingly. Moreover, you know exactly what stage of life *you're* in, what standards you're supposed to live up to, and how you're supposed to act. But without milestones, we can feel a little lost at sea.

So we talk about prolonged adolescence, Peter Pan syndrome, basement dwellers, cat ladies, and, yes, kids' tables, as blithely and unconcernedly as if we weren't talking about real people with real needs, desires, and hurts. Anyone who hasn't hit the right milestones at the right times is fair game. It's not that we're wrong to take note of these cultural phenomena and reflect on how they affect our society; the topic can hardly be ignored. What's problematic is when we overdo the shaming and the scorn, and especially when we refuse to grant grown-up people the dignity of maturity because they haven't done things at what we conceive to be the correct pace.

Here, from Janice Shaw Crouse, is a typical example of the thinking that can inspire this treatment:

> Historically, marriage has been integral to American life; as the central institution of society, marriage was the typical step forward into adulthood. Yet the marriage rate today is less than half the level of 1969. . . . A majority of people (66 percent) still live as a married couple family, but the proportion of married Americans continues to decline to levels never before seen. We must recognize that with so many women willing to engage in sex without marriage, males

have a limited incentive to "man up"—to be motivated and have a reason to accept the admittedly demanding responsibilities of adulthood.[17]

Let's not dwell on the fact that—despite the old saying that it takes two to tango—the women are getting all the blame here. (Although it demonstrates nicely some of the gender-dividing ideas and arguments that I wrote about in section 2.) Instead, let's concentrate on the idea that "historically . . . marriage was the typical step forward into adulthood." This is undeniably true. And given that it created strong families and perpetuated the human race, it was good. The trouble is here that fact is being used to make it sound as if adulthood cannot be achieved without marriage.

Just because one route to adulthood is normal and good, it doesn't necessarily follow that the road less traveled is bad and wrong. Yes, sometimes married people have to grow up fast, and single people get to take their time. But that's not always the case; just ask any single person who's been to war or taken on any other highly difficult and dangerous job. There is not just one route to maturity.

Sometimes we realize that, if life is not going to happen to us in the way we hoped it would, we have to take responsibility and create a new shape for our lives. Sometimes—like Alec Guinness with his gold watch—we create our own milestones, in our own way, and that may take just as much maturity as following the conventional path.

Perhaps you think I'm exaggerating, but consider the alternative. Many of us have known people who've stayed mired in bitterness for years, or decades, because of the lack or loss of something deeply important to them: a marriage, a child, a home. These are hard, hard situations, and it's all too easy to let them torpedo us, to give up hope and become hard, jaded, and self-centered. It takes courage, faith, and, yes, maturity to take a different path.

The long and short of it is, that single person in your pew who looks so carefree may be dealing with responsibilities and duties about which you have no idea. Maybe he or she doesn't have to take care of kids but is struggling to take care of infirm parents. Perhaps he or she is snowed under with tasks at work, or trying to mentor a troubled child, or giving freely of his or her time and money to help the church grow and flourish.

Perhaps, as I suggested in an earlier section of this book, that single person is even struggling to take care of all the tasks alone that you're able to share with a spouse.

There are many, many ways to achieve and to show maturity. Starting a family is a great one. Marriage and children give a person a crash course in selfless service, which is an integral part of the Christian faith and an absolute essential for true maturity. But selfless service isn't just for married people; in fact, Paul seems to think that single people might have special gifts and opportunities in that area. So whatever milestones we've missed, and however tricky it might be to judge exactly where we are in the maturing process, the kids' table isn't the right place for us. It might be time to start thinking about ways you can welcome the singles in your church to join you at the adults' table.

Control

We Christians today have a very odd relationship with the idea of control. We pay lip service to the idea that God has it and we don't. We sing—at least if we go to a church that still incorporates hymns into the service—"I Surrender All" and "Have Thine Own Way, Lord." We remind each other to "let go and let God."

And yet, somewhere inside ourselves, we still attempt to hang on to control for dear life.

This is something I've already touched on a couple of times in this book, in various contexts, but it's such a pervasive and influential theme in our lives and our thinking that it deserves fuller consideration. I really believe that a large part of the reason married churchgoers are often thrown for a loop by the singles is that, deep down, we are completely wedded to the idea that we should be able to control our own lives.

If a fellow Christian who's single tells you that he or she really wants to be married but hasn't been able to make it happen, it just might trigger a disbelieving or even a worried response. Because we attach such importance to marriage and family, I think a lot of churchgoers find the idea of a lack of control in these areas particularly disturbing. These are things the church considers so essential that we *have* to be able to control them; surely we can't just leave *this* up to God! (Hence those ever-popular formulae for getting God to bring you your spouse.)

But the fact is whatever control we think we have in these areas is an illusion. An examination of each step in the dating or courtship process makes this quite clear.

- We have no guarantee that someone we might be romantically interested in will come into our lives.
- A woman has no guarantee that a man she likes will ask her out.

170

- If a man asks a woman out, he has no guarantee that she will say yes. (And vice versa, for those who are okay with the woman asking the man.)
- If they do go out, neither has any guarantee that the other person will want to go out a second or third or fourth time.

And so on, and so forth. When you break it down like that, it's remarkable how little control we actually have over the process, especially in comparison with how much control we *think* we have. So much of what happens in this part of our lives depends on the decisions of someone else, and these are decisions we cannot and should not control. As Henry Cloud and John Townsend put it in their indispensable book *Boundaries*, "We are not . . . responsible for other people. Nowhere are we commanded to have 'other-control,' although we spend a lot of time and energy to get it! We are responsible *to* others and *for* ourselves."[18] In other words, we can make decisions about whom we prefer to form a romantic connection with and how we follow through, but we cannot make the other party comply with our wishes.

The fact that we actually make relatively little of this happen to ourselves—that we have so little control over it all—is a pretty terrifying lesson to learn. But it's also a healthy one. Learning this about ourselves helps uproot some of the deepest misconceptions we have about how dependent we truly are on God, how much He does for us, and how little we can do for ourselves or our loved ones.

This is another area, then, where singles have much to teach their fellow church members. By necessity, we've come to understand exactly what we can and can't control. By our example we can help demonstrate what it looks like to trust God even in those frightening areas of life in which we have little or no say.

Legacy

This is probably going to be something of a controversial statement, but here goes: I think that one of the most unchristian of all the "Christian" teachings and sayings we hear is the emphasis on leaving a legacy. You know the sort of thing I mean: "Live in such a way that there will be lots of people at your funeral." Or "You're never truly dead as long as people remember you."

And perhaps the strangest of all the arguments I've heard for marriage and childbearing: "If you don't have children, you'll be forgotten after your death."

This is anecdotal, of course, but it seems as if everyone I've known who focused on the legacy they were going to leave ended up anxious and unhappy over it. (Goodness knows when politicians start fussing about their legacy, we all end up suffering for it.) It makes me think that maybe we're not supposed to concentrate on our legacy after all, or at least we're not supposed to think about it very often.

Because overthinking our legacy can lead to some very unbiblical beliefs and practices.

For a start, it can lead us to forget some of the things that shifted between the Old Testament and the New. When we read about God's plans for the nation of Israel in the Old Testament, we find that, yes, there is a very distinct emphasis on the importance of families and inheritances and legacies. God was building a nation, defending them against their enemies, training them in obedience, and preparing them for the coming of the Messiah. Strong families were an important part of all this. They ensured that God's people, whom He had chosen, would continue on to the destiny He had prepared for them.

In the New Testament, though, things are a bit different. Now God is no longer building a nation; He's building a church. We're united not by bonds of blood but by a message that belongs to all people everywhere: the message of the gospel, which we're responsible for teaching and sharing wherever we go. Families are still important but they're not everything; spiritual connections matter even more. The church is to be one great family in which everyone, single and married alike, can find a place and be cared for, so that they're supported in doing God's work and living for Him.

In *Sex and the iWorld*, Dale S. Kuehne explains how the Bible as a whole brings these two concepts into harmony: "The Old Testament provides us with a large part of the relational matrix (marriage and family), whereas, thanks to Pentecost, the New Testament provides us with the ability to access love and integrate it into our lives and relationships and gives us a new relational community—the church."[19]

But sometimes, when the church exalts the married and puts down the single people, it can seem as if we've never moved beyond the Old Testament—as if Pentecost never happened. Mixed in with all this are some ideas that aren't even Judeo-Christian at all, exacerbating the situation even further. I'm referring to pagan ideas of fame and glory. Alastair J. Minnis, a professor of English at Yale University, explains this key difference in the two belief systems:

[In Christians' eyes] it was perfectly proper, and indeed commendable, for pagans to conceive of human fame as the final reward of their deeds, especially since, by dint of their unfavourable historical position, they were ignorant of the true glory of heaven and the true, everlasting reward. Therefore, in so far as the pagan desire for fame . . . is conducive to virtue, it may be accepted and even approved of by the Christian reader of *The Knight's Tale*. However, such a reader cannot accept either Theseus's trust in fame or his inclination to establish it as the fit objective of human endeavour. The truth of the matter is that the virtuous man should not care greatly about the perpetuity of human fame and glory after death, although charity dictates that, in the interests of his neighbours, he should not neglect fame during his lifetime.[20]

So the longing for lasting fame isn't a Christian idea at all, and yet somehow we've let it leak into our belief system and distort our ideas.

Those are some of the causes of an overemphasis on legacy; now let's look at some of its effects. For one, it can lead us to focus, to an unhealthy extent, on what other people think of us instead of focusing on trying to live for God, who we know is pleased with us simply for believing in Him (John 6:29; Heb. 11:6). It can also lead us to think those people's opinions are all that matters and cause us to be people-pleasers instead of people with healthy boundaries and firm convictions.

It can even lead us to think we can control how other people think and feel. This, I think, is the point of this quote from Dawn Eden:

Some of the advice given in fairy tales is just plain wrong. I'm thinking of that line from the film version of *The Wizard of*

174

Oz, where the Wizard, after giving the Tin Man his heart, says, "A heart is not judged by how *much you* love, but by how *much you are loved* by others."[21]

Movie lines like the one she cites—and there are plenty of them—always rub me the wrong way too. Eden goes on to explain why they bother us so much:

Those words have an inspiring sound when they are voiced in the film. But they are a lie.
    The world may judge us by how much we are loved by others. But God judges us by how much we love.[22]

This is because, however kind and loving we are to others, we have no control over how they feel about us. We can choose to love but we cannot choose for others to love us. That is a choice they have to make for themselves. This is something single people know very well—but we're not alone in that. The parent whose child rebels and turns away from him or the friend who loses a friendship through no fault of her own knows this hard truth just as surely as the single person who reaches out for romantic love but receives no response.

And just as we cannot make people love us, we cannot make people remember us. We cannot dictate how many will attend our funeral or how long our influence will last. The idea that if we love well we will be remembered well is just as misguided and just as formulaic as the idea that if we do all the right things in the right order we can attract ourselves a mate.

I've mentioned before that, for some time now, I've been working on and off on my family tree on Ancestry.com. Like many others who use the site, I've found fascinating connections to famous historical figures, some of which may actually be real. (I sincerely hope the connection I traced to Eleanor of Aquitaine is real, because honestly, how cool would that be?) But there are what I think are equally fascinating connections to be found much closer to my own generation.

For instance, there's one of my great-great-grandmothers —my mother's mother's mother's mother. I remember my great-grandmother Ella very well—she lived to be 103—but I know next to nothing about her mother. I was intrigued to discover through Ancestry that her first name was Harpalissa, a name I'd never heard before. Not too many others have either, apparently; when you Google it only a handful of instances come up. What sort of name is it—what are its ethnic roots and its meaning? And why did her parents—who gave their other daughters names like Mary, Ida, and Eva—lavish this fancy name on their second daughter? I have no idea.

Nor do I know much about her personality or about her life, beyond a bare outline. She married, had four children, and died in 1896 at the age of 38. Her youngest daughter, Ella—my great-grandmother—was not yet two at the time. She was raised by relatives and had, as far as I know, no memory of her mother.

Reading about this short life got me thinking. Harpalissa Perrine McCormack, sometimes spelled McCormick, did everything we're supposed to do if we want to be remembered, according to so much modern thinking both inside and outside the church. She married and had children. Presumably she was a loving wife and mother (and if she was anything like her female descendants, she had a stubborn streak a mile wide). But who remembers her now? As far as I know, none of my older relatives even knew her name. If there are any pictures of her in existence, I wouldn't begin to know where to look for them. She shows up in a book about the descendants of Daniel Perrin, a French Protestant who was among the first European settlers of Staten Island, but only as one name among thousands. That's it.

So when we talk so glibly about being remembered and leaving lasting legacies, we're not looking at the big picture. Does it ever really dawn on us that those "lasting legacies" probably won't last beyond a couple of generations? Obviously we'd realize it if we stopped a minute to think seriously about it, but do we? And does it make a difference in our values and priorities?

Let's face it: those who *are* remembered past a few generations are rarely remembered for the reasons that we now say people will be remembered. Their legacies often have very little to do with what kind of family man or homemaker they were. My (possible) ancestor Eleanor of Aquitaine is a great example. Today she's remembered for (1) royal status, (2) a life that was colorful in the extreme, and (3) being played by Katharine Hepburn in a great classic film. Most of us have few if any of those factors working in our favor.

Here's another example: in pursuit of my hobby as a Charles Dickens fanatic, I've met a few of the great man's descendants. They do wonderful work writing books about their famous ancestor, or traveling the world doing one-man shows of his stories, or finding other ways to help promote his memory and his writings. But if it weren't for his already great fame as an author, they wouldn't know their ancestor's name any more than I know mine. They probably wouldn't have the strong family relationships that they do, either; they wouldn't be getting together for big gatherings with their fourth and fifth and sixth cousins, any more than I do with mine.

Granted, we have the internet now, which my great-great-great-grandmother didn't. Maybe that will help future generations to know more about ours—but probably not an awful lot more. Most of us, however much time we spend chatting on Facebook or Twitter or Tumblr, don't have the kind of significant online presence that will tell a future great-great-great-grandchild much about our lives. Despite the saying that nothing ever really disappears from the internet, there's still something of an ephemeral quality to much of what we do and say there.

So we come back to this inescapable truth: most of us won't be remembered for long, whether we have children or not. So why do we talk as if we will? More than that, why do we talk as if it matters?

Could it be that, deep down, we're frightened of our own mortality?

It's not unforgivable if we are. I doubt there's ever been a human being on earth who hasn't experienced that chilling fear at least once or twice. Even Jesus did. But the cure for that fear isn't scrambling to find ways to make posterity remember our names or our influence. It's recalling our ultimate goal: eternity in heaven. In light of the genuine immortality that will be ours, earthly immortality no longer looks quite as important as it did.

C. S. Lewis offers a helpful take on these ideas in *The Great Divorce*, with his tale of an artist who arrives in heaven and wants to meet other "distinguished" artists. His guide explains:

> "They aren't distinguished—no more than anyone else. Don't you understand? The Glory flows into everyone, and back from everyone: like light and mirrors. But the light's the thing."

"Do you mean there are no famous men?"

"They are all famous. They are all known, remembered, recognised by the only Mind that can give a perfect judgment." . . .

"One must be content with one's reputation among posterity, then," said the Ghost.

"My friend," said the Spirit. "Don't you know?"

"Know what?"

"That you and I are already completely forgotten on the Earth?"[23]

If you remember the story, you know the artist doesn't take this news at all well. Which is both ridiculous and tragic, when you think of how unimportant his earthly reputation really was in light of the tremendous good news the Spirit gave him: that in heaven we are all known. *Really* known.

In the final analysis, maybe that's what we're really thinking about when we worry about being remembered: our deep need to be known as we are, to know that someone sees us and cares for us, that we have made an impression. This is a need we all share, married people and single people alike. The good news for Christians is that we have a God who does know and care deeply. But sometimes it's hard to remember that when we can't see His face or feel His touch. Those are the times when we need each other—and that's one of the reasons He gave us the church.

ELEVEN

WHAT THE CHURCH GETS RIGHT

For the most part, I would say that the church has been supportive of me as a single. One good example is the Bible studies that I have been to. . . . I found incredible support among my friends and peers in those studies. Having like-minded people to share in the struggles helps immensely.—Scott

I'm deeply grateful to be a Christian, because my relationship with Christ has not only given me the consolation I need as a single person but also helped me stay focused on the habit of self-gift that I will need should I ever find a husband, rather than becoming hardened in the ways of living only for myself.—Kathleen

I've spent quite some time now writing about the difficulties of single life within the church. In the process, I've cited a number of secular sources, ideas, and alternatives. At this point, it would be completely understandable if you were starting to wonder about my belief in and commitment to the church. If the church has let me down in so many ways, why am I still here? If I get so much out of secular sources, why not give up on the church entirely and find help and guidance elsewhere?

If those are your questions, they're very good ones. The answer is a simple one on the surface, though it will take some time to unpack. The simple part of it is this: I'm still here because I need the church. I need it desperately.

> From that time many of His disciples went back and walked with Him no more. Then Jesus said to the twelve, "Do you also want to go away?"
>
> But Simon Peter answered Him, "Lord, to whom shall we go? You have the words of eternal life." (John 6:66–68)

I've come back to those verses many times over the course of my spiritual journey. In a nutshell, they explain why all of us, even those who have been let down and hurt, need the church. I don't write these words lightly. I have heard many, many stories of people who have left the church because of abuse, betrayal, or false and manipulative teachings and have not been able to bring themselves to go back. I respect their feelings and I ache at the thought of what they've been through.

But I still say, as respectfully and sympathetically as I know how, that Christians need the church. More than that: Christians *are* the church. We can't help being part of it, wherever we are, however hard we've tried to leave it behind us. Jesus Christ has "the words of eternal life," and He established the church, going so far as to call it His body. Each of us who believes in Him is part of that body.

And when we are functioning as He designed us to function, the church reflects His truth, goodness, and love. We have been given a mission to accomplish, but it's not just to promote a message, as important as that is. It's also to live in relationship with one another—in the kind of relationships that demonstrate God's love to a broken and hurting world. "By this all will know that you are My disciples," Jesus told us, "if you have love for one another" (13:35).

For more than two thousand years, the church has carried out that mission. Yes, sometimes we mess it up quite badly. Yes, we are imperfect people trying to reflect a perfect love, and that doesn't always go so well. But we've survived this long. We must be doing something right. More than that— we must have been guided and sustained by Someone far stronger, wiser, and better than we are.

That's why, despite mistakes and missteps, the church still has much to offer single people. Yes, there is much work to be done and many walls still to be broken down to integrate singles fully into today's family-oriented church. I've already talked about some practical steps to take in that direction, and I'll be talking about that more in a little while. But right now I want to talk about what the church is already doing right and encourage more of the same.

First and foremost, of course, the church offers us what it offers everyone: the opportunity to worship, learn, and serve in community with our fellow Christians. This is no small thing. It's what every Christian needs, and it's what keeps many Christians coming back even when their particular church experiences have been frustrating and difficult. As C. S. Lewis wrote in a discussion of his own reluctance to go to church when he first came to faith:

God can show Himself as He really is only to real men. And that means not simply to men who are individually good, but to men who are united together in a body, loving one another, helping one another, showing Him to one another. For that is what God meant humanity to be like; like players in one band, or organs in one body.[1]

This is what the church has to offer all Christians. But what does it have to offer single people specifically?

Higher Standards

I wrote in an earlier chapter about what a difficult and lonely business it can be for single people to follow church teachings in a time when we get so little encouragement or help in doing so. However, in some ways, the expectation that we follow those teachings brings with it its own reward. When the whole world seems to be obsessed with sex—and believe me, when you're not having sex, that is something you're very much aware of—the church of God gives us something the world can't. Those teachings and expectations remind us that we don't *have* to be obsessed with sex . . . and in a paradoxical way, they set us free. They help us stay off the crazy, broken merry-go-round of hookups and one-night stands and relationships with no real depth or foundation.

I'm not saying it's all a picnic in the park. We've seen that the church has its own problems when it comes to helping establish a healthy singles scene. What I am saying is when the church teaches sexuality based on the Word of God, and even more when it helps hold us accountable for following those teachings, it gives us something important and valuable—something that's very hard to find outside the church. At a minimum, it helps us take a more thoughtful, balanced, well-rounded approach to relationships.

Additionally, it offers us a place where that approach is seen as good and right, not freakish and weird. That just might be the most valuable aspect of all. Because when sex outside of marriage is so prevalent and so normalized, there is just one kind of behavior between adults of consenting age that is looked at askance: not having sex.[2] According to this culture, it's all very well to wait a while, to have your first time be with someone you really care about . . . but there's always an underlying assumption that this person will come along in plenty of time to save you from doing something really embarrassing like waiting far too long. To put it in terms of what Hollywood shows us, remember that *The 40-Year-Old Virgin* wasn't just a movie title; it was a punch line. I believe that, if polled, the vast majority in the entertainment industry would tell you that they don't even believe such a thing exists. Or that if it does, it shouldn't.

Frankly, secular culture can be absolutely merciless to the single and/or celibate person. You don't have to spend much time on Twitter, for example, to learn that accusing someone of being single—or, even worse, a virgin—is one of the most insulting things you can do. That accusation carries with it the connotation that you're unwanted and unworthy, so it's no wonder that no one has ever desired you. Against such an insult there is no defense—unless, of course, you have a strong enough self-image to stand up against it and know deep inside that it isn't true.

And there is nothing that gives a person a stronger self-image than knowing he or she is God's beloved creation, made in *His* image, redeemed by His sacrifice.

This knowledge is one of the most precious, most valuable gifts my faith has given me. I'm not talking just in terms of my sexuality now; this is a knowledge that applies to and enhances every aspect of life. It came originally from the pages of God's Word, but this belief would not be nearly so strong—it might not even have lasted this long—had it not been reinforced in me all my life by Christian pastors and teachers and friends and the Christian community in general. In other words, by the church.

Whatever mistakes the church has made, however we fail to live up to our own ideals and standards, we have this belief as our foundation, and wherever this is the case—wherever we as a community have this truth embedded within us—it will always give us a measure of strength, sanity, and spiritual health. These qualities and the reason for them are something the world can't grasp without the help of the Holy Spirit, and so they're certainly not something the world has to offer us outside of the church. As Jesus told His disciples, "Not as the world gives do I give to you" (14:27).

Of course we're only human, so even this great gift of belief doesn't mean we'll never struggle. That's where another gift of the church, a gift that I've already hinted at, is so important. That is the gift of Christian community.

Community of Believers

Now, as I've explained, our community could be doing much better than it is, in part because there are barriers between married people and singles in the church that need to be dismantled. But even where those barriers are especially strong and high, single people of faith are not without community within the church. It offers us a unique setting for us to come together and share our particular struggles, and in the process build each other up.

There's a joke in some Christian circles that if you get a bunch of singles together for long enough, you'll end up with a bunch of singles complaining that they can't find anybody to date. Admittedly, there's a lot of truth in this (though the jokers don't always realize that some of their own teachings, like the ones we covered in section 2, have a lot to do with it!). But whatever our shortcomings and difficulties in the area of romance, many of us have learned to build strong, lasting Christian friendships—and that is no small thing. Those friendships often become the support systems that are there for us in times of need or of celebration, the family of God actively working in our lives.

Honestly, I never met a ton of guys at church that I felt were super solid, so I never saw youth group or my college ministry that I attended as a place to meet people to date. Though it was helpful to see how friend-ships could be formed in such a setting and that guys could be encouraging to girls and vice versa even if they weren't romantically interested. These settings were often a really fun time of being with guys and girls, but not having to worry about being lonely because you weren't dating anyone.—Allison

And there's another very valuable aspect to such com-munity: the better we get to know our brothers and sisters in Christ, really know them in real life, the more we're inoculated against some of the dangerous and misleading teachings and theories on gender I wrote about earlier. You can't seriously believe all men are oppressive or all women are leeches when you have close Christian friendships with real men and real women. You may be tempted to believe those things in moments of weakness or frustration, but you have something tangible to keep you grounded in the truth that both genders have virtues and strengths as well as great flaws, and the world isn't completely full of vicious, feral members of the opposite sex just panting for their chance to take you down—and that you don't enter into a romantic relationship just to see how subservient you can get the other person to be toward you but rather for both of you to learn to serve each other with love, patience, and humility.

In the best churches—the ones that don't give in to fads, fears, and falsehoods but remain solidly rooted in scriptural truth—that message comes from the top down: the pastor preaches it, the leaders reinforce it, and the congregation learns to live it in their day-to-day lives. It may not mean that the singles suddenly start pairing off like the animals on their way to Noah's ark, but it often does mean that they receive the gift of strong teaching, good examples to follow, and a healthy, supportive community.

Ultimately, through the blessing of solid church leaders and teaching, I have come to respect, admire, and appreciate women more than I ever would have on my own—or certainly [more] than I would have by listening to the messages of pop culture.—Travis

I sat through a series of sermons on the responsibilities a man has within his family, and I came to a much deeper understanding of how hard it is to be a godly

man. This has given me an immense amount of respect for the opposite sex.—Charity

I would say the church has helped me to realize that men should not be looked at as a "savior" for loneliness or for validation and are not responsible for my happiness.—Nichole

When we are given such gifts in our churches, it's harder to let bitterness grow in our souls. We single people may still need to come to terms with the death of dreams and grieve our losses, but we can learn to do so in healthy, God-honoring ways. Our trust in God and His church can thrive even when we can't understand why we've been denied many of the things we've longed for.

◆　◆　◆

There's a passage in one of my favorite books, Charles Dickens's *Little Dorrit*, that I've often held on to when tempted to lose faith and hope. I love this passage because it shows so beautifully what it looks like to keep believing in God's goodness even when we feel that it's far from us. Dickens is writing about a character who has lived a life full of harsh treatment and disappointment, and yet . . .

He was a dreamer in such wise, because he was a man who had, deep-rooted in his nature, a belief in all the gentle and good things his life had been without. Bred in meanness and hard dealing, this had rescued him to be a man of honourable mind and open hand. Bred in coldness and severity, this had rescued him to have a warm and sympathetic heart. Bred in a creed too darkly audacious to pursue, through its process of reversing the making of man in the image of his Creator

188

to the making of his Creator in the image of an erring man, this had rescued him to judge not, and in humility to be merciful, and to have hope and charity.

And this saved him still from the whimpering weakness and cruel selfishness of holding that because such a happiness or such a virtue had not come into his little path, or worked well for him, therefore it was not in the great scheme, but was reducible, when found in appearance, to the basest elements. A disappointed mind he had, but a mind too firm and healthy for such unwholesome air. Leaving himself in the dark, it could rise into the light, seeing it shine on others and hailing it.

Therefore, he sat before his dying fire, sorrowful to think upon the way by which he had come to that night, yet not strewing poison on the way by which other men had come to it.[3]

Dickens once wrote to a correspondent that he tried to put the spirit of the New Testament into his works and characters, and I believe that we're seeing that here.[4] "A belief in all the gentle and good things his life had been without," I think, is a strong indicator of a Christian worldview at work. But it's not always easy even for the most devout Christians to maintain such a belief on their own. This is another thing that a supportive Christian community can help us do. Again, from my observation, this is a quality of Christian friendships and communities that can be very hard to find in the wider world.

Shared Redemption

In fact, I think of this fallen world rather like a broken mirror. As some of my illustrations and anecdotes have shown, you can still see little pieces of God's beauty, purpose, and goodness reflected in the shards. Glimpses of truth flash out at us sometimes. But it can be very difficult to find consistent expressions of this truth and goodness in the secular culture. The mirror is still broken, after all.

There are those who think that the more traditional, conservative parts of our culture are less broken than the rest. I once thought so myself. But if that was ever true, I think it's much less true than it was. "Liberal vs. conservative" seems to have little to do with the matter, especially in the area of love and marriage. In the secular world these days, there are fewer fundamental differences between the two worldviews than some of us would like to believe.

Here's an example. Last Valentine's Day, a new romantic comedy came out called *How to Be Single*. When I first saw the poster at my local movie theater, I winced. I knew instinctively, from many years of experience, that modern Hollywood's version of the single life was going to be so many worlds apart from my own lifestyle and ideals it might as well be in a different galaxy. I needn't have felt concerned over it, I suppose—I had no interest in seeing the movie, and there were plenty of other films out there to see—except that it felt like just one more addition to the debased, sex-drenched image of singleness the entertainment industry is constantly putting out there into the world. And, as a single person, that does concern me.

Sure enough, the movie was rated R for sexual content and profanity, and the tagline read in part, "Sleeping around in the city that never sleeps was never so much fun." Though I never did see *How to Be Single*, the reviews all confirmed it was the same old raunchy comedy we've grown used to seeing in recent years, only with more people staying single at the end of it. There was meant to be an empowering message somewhere in there, I take it—the idea that you can be single and still have a good life. And as you know, I'm all in favor of that idea in principle. But when "the good life" largely means a never-ending round of partying, drinking, and sex, I feel as if that message has been undermined. Because I don't believe those are the things that bring lasting satisfaction in life.

But that's just liberal Hollywood for you, right? What do they know about it anyway? A traditionalist conservative would give you a much better idea of what the good life should look like for a single person . . . right?

Well, if you go looking on the Web for romantic advice for and from conservatives, here's a sample of what you might find:

> Conservative activist Lisa De Pasquale suggesting that maybe other conservative women shouldn't let appearances get in the way of sex on the first date.[5]
>
> Fox News "sexpert" Dr. Yvonne Kristin Fulbright listing some of the reasons why sex on the first date is a bad idea . . . and then suggesting that "anywhere from four to nine weeks" before sex works fine for some.[6]
>
> The *Washington Times* reporting, regarding sexual behavior and attitudes, that "the gap between the two groups was hardly enormous: 49 percent of conservative Republicans said they have had a one-night stand, compared to 65 percent of liberal Democrats."[7]

It seems that, in the mainstream, the conservative worldview has caught up with the liberal worldview in many areas.

I take no pleasure in saying this; I'm conservative myself. I have been since I was twelve years old. But without faith, it appears even a conservative worldview is not enough to guide one through the swamps of the modern singles scene. Many conservatives appear to have fallen for the lie that marriage and family are so important that you're justified in doing anything you can in the search for a mate.

You're probably starting to get the picture by now: this culture we're living in is not conducive to living lives of faith and principle. What single people of faith need, then, is help in living counterculturally. That, by definition, is something the wider culture will never help us find. I'm not just talking about the sex-on-the-first-date thing now; I'm talking about learning to be people of character and learning to look for spouses of character.

Believe me when I say this is a desperate need for single Christians—for single people in general, actually. I've had a few chances to see what it looks like out there on the secular singles scene, and it did not fill me with inspiration or confidence.

I would not want to date a non-Christian now. I was married nineteen years when I was still an unbeliever. I experienced so many things that can deteriorate and dissolve a marriage, including the final step of divorce. That's not an experience I want to relive. My beliefs now are that God has a plan for my life and has my future in His hands.—Jim

The Meetup groups and online singles groups I've joined, on the off chance of finding a man of faith and morals hanging out with the movie-watching or novel-reading or swing-dancing or "Mystery Science Theater 3000"–loving crowd, are full of the burned-out, the jaded, the self-loathing, and the hopeless. I don't mean to make sweeping generalizations, because there are good guys out there too, but so many of the men I've met in these groups never seem to even consider looking for a woman of character or substance. Then they tell you all about the woman who lived with them for six months, absconded with their money, and left them wallowing in misery.

In short, it's not a pretty picture.

As Christians, in many of these groups we can sometimes feel like a member of a different species. I don't mean a superior species, just a different one. Our fundamental values, goals, and lifestyles are in direct opposition in many ways. Beyond the surface hobbies and likings we share—things that do matter to us but aren't enough in themselves to form the basis for deep and sustainable relationships—we scrabble to find common ground.

When we're among our Christian friends, on the other hand, we may have major disagreements, but way down deep, at a certain level, we tend to get each other. We have something crucial in common, something that puts us on the same page, something that has transformed the way we think, speak, act, and live. We have redemption through Christ and the indwelling Holy Spirit.

And this is not just something that makes for a bunch of individual relationships between God and each of us. As blogger Joel J. Miller writes, "We don't get Jesus to ourselves, and we shouldn't want him by ourselves. Jesus is best known—really only known—in community."[8] Christian community, as found in a healthy church, encourages not only the growth of Christian character within each of us but also the growth of Christian love between us.

This is what the church, at its best, offers single people. In the absence of marriage and children, many of us rely strongly on the community we find within the body of Christ to help fill the empty spaces in our lives and meet the deep needs of our souls. We have a rare and special gift in this kind of community, one that many of us are deeply grateful for. Yes, it has flaws, but it also has great strengths.

TWELVE

◆ ◆ ◆

WE NEED EACH OTHER

I personally have dealt with my never being married. After years of asking why and crying or getting angry, I have felt pretty content. I have accepted the way the church is toward me. I had no issues at all . . . until I went to lunch with a single lady—never married—no kids.

She broke into tears and I saw myself all over again. It broke my heart. I knew and she knew she had no support from the church, no one that genuinely wanted to hear her struggles. At that point, I knew I had to start speaking up.—Carole

I touched earlier on the secular singles scene and the bleak prospect it offers. I want to go back to that topic for a few minutes. Looking at what's going on with single people in the mainstream, and more specifically at what's missing from their lives, gives us a clue as to what single people are looking for from the church—and, more surprisingly, what single people have to offer the church.

That singles scene, in fact, has been much in the news lately. Sometimes I think our society spends half its time hooking up and the other half writing about it. There's been a flood of articles in recent months examining the hookup culture, the reasons behind it, and the effects it's having on its participants and on the culture in general.

In the fall of 2015 came *Vanity Fair*'s much-buzzed-about piece "Tinder and the Dawn of the 'Dating Apocalypse.'" Nancy Jo Sales talked with a number of men and women all over the country who are devotees of the popular dating app, and she painted a bleak picture indeed: men "racking up girls," maybe two or three a week (or even two or three a night!), and then never seeing any of them again. Women feeling used and "devalued," hungering even for a text from guys whom they know in the back of their minds just want them for one quick hookup. People in bars "peering into their screens and swiping on the faces of strangers they may have sex with later that evening." People so afraid of getting hurt that they don't dare try having a real, lengthy relationship but so afraid of one-night stands that they have to get "blackout drunk" first. Sexual encounters that turn aggressive, with guys who've watched too much porn and, according to one interviewee, "have a skewed view of the reality of sex."

It all culminated in scenes like this:

[Alex] says that he himself has slept with five different women he met on Tinder—"Tinderellas," the guys call them—in the last eight days. Dan and Marty, also Alex's roommates in a shiny high-rise apartment building near Wall Street, can vouch for that. In fact, they can remember whom Alex has slept with in the past week more readily than he can.

"Brittany, Morgan, Amber," Marty says, counting on his fingers. "Oh, and the Russian—Ukrainian?"

"Ukrainian," Alex confirms. "She works at—" He says the name of a high-end art auction house. Asked what these women are like, he shrugs. "I could offer a résumé, but that's about it . . . works at J. Crew; senior at Parsons; junior at Pace; works in finance . . ."

"We don't know what the girls are like," Marty says.

"And they don't know us," says Alex.[1]

It was a grim tale, a *danse macabre* going on and on with no relief in sight. Understandably, the article caused widespread concern among its readers. Any number of factors were blamed for the debacle, from demographics to technology to feminism to toxic masculinity to the recession to practically anything else you can think of. Much the same was true of another article that appeared several months later in *Quartz*, written by a recent graduate of Middlebury College about the hookup scene she had experienced there.

This piece was titled, poignantly, "Most Women Don't Enjoy Hookup Culture—So Why Do We Force Ourselves to Participate?" In it, Leah Fessler wrote:

The popular media most frequently characterizes hookup culture as a series of emotionless one-night stands. At Middlebury, such casual hookups definitely occur.

Far more frequent, however, were pseudo-relationships, the mutant children of meaningless sex and loving partnerships. Two students consistently hook up with one another—and typically, only each other—for weeks, months, even years. Yet per unspoken social code, neither party is permitted emotional involvement, commitment, or vulnerability. To call them exclusive would be "clingy," or even "crazy."[2]

Fessler eventually ended up doing her senior thesis on the "pseudo-relationships" that were causing her and her friends such frustration. She made a very interesting discovery: namely, that hardly anyone involved in Middlebury's hookup scene *wanted* to be involved in Middlebury's hookup scene. Most of them wanted committed relationships. But in the milieu in which they found themselves, they had no idea how to get there. Most of these bright young adults literally did not know how to go on a date and could not seem to find anyone who knew how, either.

Fessler writes tellingly that when she was hesitating on the brink of joining the hookup scene as a freshman, "the [only] alternative seemed to me to be abstinence." So she plunged in, and had years of unfulfilling casual sex instead. Being younger and more optimistic than the *Vanity Fair* writer and her interviewees, Fessler believes things can and should change and suggests ways that this could happen. Mostly, her suggestions involve women eschewing the kind of feminism that tells them that sex without emotional attachment is the way to go; getting in touch with their own bodies and feelings; and advocating "pleasure-centered sex ed."[3]

Most traditional Christians would take a sharply opposing view. Believing that sex is intended for marriage, we would suggest that this generation is dealing with the still-radioactive fallout of the sexual revolution and that simply coming up with better, more thoughtful, more engaged ways to have sex is only putting a Band-Aid on the problem. (There are some who would go further and blame the college setting specifically, but given that we see much the same pattern among those who don't go to college, that critique doesn't really hold water.) But if we leave it there, we don't actually get any nearer to the root of the problem than Fessler did. That is, we miss the underlying cause that propels young men and women into the hookup scene when it's not really what they want and causes them to embrace a sexual ethic that leads to emptiness. I have a theory about this. Maybe it's too simplistic, but I think I can tell you why all this is happening in three words: fear of loneliness.

Facing Fear

I submit that fear of loneliness is, if not *the* driving force of our time, at least one of the great driving forces. Recall Leah Fessler's words—that among her peers on that college campus, it was either hooking up or abstinence. And abstinence was unacceptable. Why? She doesn't spell it out, but I'm pretty sure I can guess: because abstinence would cut her off from any hope of a romantic relationship at all. Socially speaking, she would be isolated, separate, alone. And that would lead to loneliness.

She's not the only one. Way down deep, I think, most of us struggle with this fear. Ultimately it's what makes it so very hard to deal with the prospect of going through life without ever marrying. It's one reason why so many married Christians think and speak of singleness as the unthinkable fate, like Leslie Ludy when she wrote about her dread of sitting alone for the rest of her life wearing a burlap sack or whatever it was. It's why many even feel a sort of fear around older single people. I confess I felt that fear sometimes when I was younger; some of my friends have confessed to feeling it too.

But maybe we're looking at it all wrong. Maybe there's a lot the church can learn from people who face the tough prospect of lifelong singleness, who wrestle with the feelings of aloneness and isolation it can bring. Maybe the very people to help teach the church how to prepare for and deal with the fear of loneliness are the ones who know it intimately.

I'm not saying that married people never know loneliness. Many of them have told me that they do, and I believe it. Being in a relationship as close as marriage and yet feeling emotionally estranged from one's spouse must be a special kind of pain, and I have nothing but sympathy for those who experience it.

But single people know a unique kind of loneliness. And I think that deep down most of us realize that. Just the other day I was talking with a friend about someone we both knew who was going through a divorce, and she told me that this woman had just joined eHarmony. I nodded knowingly. We'd both seen this before: the moment when a new divorcée or widow suddenly recognizes the approach of aloneness. In the case of divorcées, at least, they theoretically know it's coming, and if the relationship was really bad, with abuse or adultery or other mistreatment going on, they even know that it's got to be better than what they've left behind. But be that as it may, the moment comes when panic hits. And you can tell because the person usually starts looking frantically at dating sites.

Getting out of a dangerous marriage may be justified, even necessary, but with the escape comes a loss that the person often hasn't really thought through: the loss of close proximity to another person, even if it was only physical nearness. And with that loss can come another kind of loss: the loss of close friendships, including those within the church. Both the divorced and the widowed can experience this. We've already talked about how divorcées in church are sometimes made to feel as if they bear a stain that can never be washed off. And as for widows, Miriam Neff wrote in *Christianity Today*, "Studies show that widows lose 75 percent of their friendship network when they lose a spouse. . . . One pastor described us by saying we move from the front row of the church to the back, and then out the door."[4]

These losses are real and significant ones. And let's face it: they're losses that most people will face someday, even those in long and happy marriages. Someday, most of us will be faced with aloneness. Some, like my father's friend who lost his wife and children, will spend many years alone. For many of us, it's our worst nightmare.

But what helps us deal with that nightmare is not scolding and pontificating about the decay of marriage and the prevalence of singleness. What helps is watching people reach out and take care of each other as Christians are supposed to do. My father did this for his widowed friend, driving him to the hospital for his surgery and visiting him frequently while he was there—even while he also had to care for my mother, who happened to be recovering from her own surgery at the same time. Other members of their bluegrass group did the same, calling and visiting their friend during his recovery. Seeing them come forward to support and care for this man did my heart more good than all the handwringing about demographic trends I've ever seen. It gives me hope that one day, when I need it, there will be people who do the same for me.

Columnist Gaye Clark also offers examples of how Christians ministered to her in loving, practical ways after she was widowed:

> Months after my husband, Jim, died, an ice storm crippled our city. Power outages citywide and downed trees littered homes and businesses. The damage was so widespread that I couldn't possibly ask church friends to leave their own homes to address mine. But leave they did. A tree had fallen through the roof of one church friend's home, yet he and his dad headed first to my place. "I'm waiting on the insurance company to call me," he said. "I can wait here working a chainsaw as easily as pace the floor there." . . .
>
> After my husband's death, two of his friends—one an accountant, the other a senior bank vice president—helped me work out a budget based on my lower income level. And these two did not treat me like an obligation. Every time they left my home, a piece of my burden went with them.[5]

Another thing that helps is watching older single people live rich and fulfilling lives. The first time I remember having the chance to do this is when I was in college. Because I minored in music, I took piano lessons every semester from an older single woman who was an assistant professor of music there. She was always talking about her performing and teaching experiences, including multiple trips to Europe. She could chat knowledgeably and appreciatively with me about *The Phantom of the Opera* as well as Mozart. I wasn't then worried about lifelong singleness myself, but it did dawn on me somewhere in there that lifelong singleness the way my teacher did it might not be a bad thing. And I've often recalled that impression in the years since.

◆ ◆ ◆

These are the things that help single people learn to face and deal with fear and loneliness. And the church as a whole can benefit from what we've learned along the way. Perhaps there's room in the church for a ministry staffed entirely by single people for the purpose of reaching out to help the soon-to-be singles. Because we live every day where so many people are afraid to go. And we're surviving. We can tell them, and mean it, "This is doable. I'm doing it. You can too."

It's not just divorcées and widows who can learn from singles, either. We're uniquely placed to help all of our fellow Christians learn more about trusting God. We've had to learn to rely on Him when no one else was there; we've had to believe He heard our cries when no one else did. For us, "all you need is Jesus" isn't just a nice slogan. It's the truth we live by. When you reach a certain age and you have none of the people in your life that you thought you'd have—no spouse, no children—then you really know how to speak those words and mean them.

Beyond just living with loneliness, as I mentioned earlier, at times many of us have actively had to choose it—a choice that goes against every instinct human beings have and everything our culture promotes. Practically everywhere we go these days, from the classroom to the movie theater, we're taught to be people of action, to make the bold choices, to "follow our hearts," to grab what we want when we want it, and to never just give it up and walk away—even if walking away might be better for us. Practically every TV show has to show people making the stupidest choices possible, because to back off and *not* choose something stupid just wouldn't make for good drama. (No wonder so much of Hollywood doesn't believe that virgins exist.)

What Dorothy L. Sayers once called "the doctrine of snatch" is absolutely pervasive in our society.[6] And that makes sense in a time when more and more families are breaking up, more institutions are disintegrating, and the possibility of being alone scares us so badly. In such a time, even the wrong relationships can look better than no relationship at all.

As theologian Stanley Hauerwas puts it:

> Community by itself cannot overwhelm the loneliness of our lives. I think we are a culture that produces extreme loneliness. Loneliness creates a hunger—and hunger is the right word, indicating as it does the physical character of the desire and need to touch another human being. But such desperate loneliness is very dangerous.[7]

With all this going on, single Christians who trust and obey God, who make wise and careful decisions out of obedience and love for Him, are fish very much out of water. The Tinder scene is so removed from us, or we're so removed from it, that we're like those people in old novels who couldn't get into "society" and had to stand on the outside looking in. It's ironic that our free-and-easy age is just as stringent about who gets to be part of society as those rule-bound, hidebound Victorians and Edwardians.

It's a bit like being the hapless Lily Bart in Edith Wharton's *The House of Mirth*, who makes up her mind over and over again to make the kind of ethical compromises that will let her become part of the wealthy, sophisticated society around her only to be repeatedly yanked back at the last minute by an inconvenient conscience. The trouble is:

> If one were not a part of the season's fixed routine, one swung unsphered in a void of social non-existence. Lily, for all her dissatisfied dreaming, had never really conceived the possibility of revolving about a different centre: it was easy enough to despise the world, but decidedly difficult to find any other habitable region.[8]

So maybe single Christians *and* married Christians can help each other learn to live counterculturally in a world where we often find ourselves on the outside. But in order for this to happen, single Christians need to be allowed more of a voice in the church. As Hauerwas goes on to say, "It is not community for its own sake that we seek. Rather, we should try to be a definite *kind* of community."[9] For single Christians to choose the right kind of community and to benefit it with their presence and insights, we have to be allowed to truly belong.

Represent!

These days, *representation* is a watchword in our culture as we talk about how to feature more minority viewpoints everywhere from our businesses to our TV shows. Representation is something the church needs to think about too—and one of the groups that needs to be represented is single people. The more we're integrated into the mainstream of church life, the more chance we have to serve, to participate, and to make ourselves heard and add an important perspective to the conversation. And that perspective is needed throughout the church, from top to bottom.

The world looks at believers differently from nonbelievers. We are put up for all to see, and for those that are not in a relationship, we are singled out and watched more closely.—Veronica

Singles are often shunted off to their own Bible studies, dinner groups, and fellowship times, and in some churches have their own separate worship service. They often are not considered for or allowed to serve in leadership positions.—Fiona

The *New York Times* featured a story in 2011 on single pastors who were having trouble finding jobs because of their singleness. One man they talked to, Mark Almlie, had applied for more than five hundred jobs.

> Mr. Almlie, 37, has been shocked, he says, at what he calls unfair discrimination, based mainly on irrational fears: that a single pastor cannot counsel a mostly married flock, that he might sow turmoil by flirting with a church member, or that he might be gay. [Another man, Matt Steen,] encountered concerns about the possibility of sexual misconduct during the year he fruitlessly sought a new position as a youth pastor. . . . Many interviewers seemed to fear that he might "do something stupid, like get involved with a student," he said.[10]

Pretty ironic when you think about how many sex scandals in the church have involved married people rather than singles.

I don't know anything about the churches that expressed these views, but I can make a few educated guesses about what's going on in them where single people are concerned. Maybe you can too, by now. More than likely, they are churches where single people have their place—but their place is narrowly defined and seldom allows them to assume positions of authority or influence.

It seems to me that many of these suspicions might have been allayed if single people were fully integrated into the life of those churches. If, for instance, they were on the search committees that found, interviewed, and voted on the pastoral candidates. Or if single people had ever held pastoral positions there themselves.

It's like Christena Cleveland said: we tend to trust those who have had life experiences similar to our own. With others we're wary, seeing flaws and disadvantages before we see things we might have in common. It takes an extra effort to see people who are different from us as people who still might be qualified for leadership, regardless. Our default is to wonder, like those worried about marital counseling, "But how can that person meet my needs?" instead of getting creative and, say, getting someone else to do the counseling, or having the occasional guest speaker do marriage sermons . . . or even trusting that a wise single pastor may have powers of observation, imagination, and empathy that might qualify him or her to speak a few words on the subject now and then.

But we can start, first, by seeing singles as people who are good at working in the nursery, at singing or playing in the music ministry, at working with the elderly or the needy, at organizing or running events, and concentrating on the qualities and gifts that allow them to do these things so well. And second, by asking how those qualities and gifts might benefit the church in even greater ways and finding ways to help single people develop their gifts to their fullest extent—perhaps by mentoring them or encouraging them to engage in further study . . . or even asking them to serve on search committees. In other words, by giving them the same opportunities and encouragement we would give married people.

I would implore the church to place a greater emphasis on mentorship and discipleship so that young men and women are equipped to serve and lead—married or single.—Travis

After all, when we do bring up singleness in church, it's often to point to the Bible verses saying that single people have more time and energy to serve, and fewer distractions. That being the case, why not take full advantage of it? Why not encourage single people to serve in *all* capacities?

This is the sort of long-term change that needs to happen at the institutional level. But long-term change takes time. We can't just sit around forever waiting for someone to instigate massive change; we all have to start doing what we can do in our own spheres. In fact, long-term institutional change needs to start with immediate, individual changes.

Learn to Listen

At my church last year, several of us participated in a small group led by the pastor, a "task force" dedicated to learning about how to help the church function more as an extended family to those in need of one. It was a great group, made up of people in all stages of life. (I would recommend this kind of group to other churches—among other things, it's a wonderful way for single people and married people to start to get to know each other and understand each other's concerns.)

We read Wesley J. Hill's *Spiritual Friendship* and Dale S. Kuehne's *Sex in the iWorld* and had some long, serious, refreshing talks about what the church was doing well and what it needed to do differently. Nothing was (theoretically) off the table, so some ideas were quite radical: people moving to be closer to each other, people foregoing moving away for work to stay close to the church, and so forth.

While there's a lot to be said for brainstorming and the "nothing off the table" style of conversation, I couldn't help but feel after a while that this mode of thinking had some disadvantages. For one thing, it seemed too focused on the large scale and not enough on what we could start doing right away. During one of these sessions, I broke in to make a point: yes, it was interesting and enlightening and helpful to talk about the crucial role of the church in our lives and what kind of major sacrifices and commitments we should all be willing to make in order to start changing things . . . but just now I would be happy if more people would make the time to talk to me at the coffee hour after Sunday morning services.

You see, integration starts simply by letting down our barriers, looking around, and letting people into our lives. It can mean stopping and talking to someone new instead of making a beeline for the same group you talk to every Sunday, or maybe even inviting that someone to join the group on a regular basis. It can mean making a conscious choice to ask single people to do the Scripture readings, make the announcements . . . or even light the Advent candles! It can mean, when you invite a few couples for lunch, thinking to invite a few singles along as well.

It can mean that, at the time of greeting during the church service, instead of turning to hug our own family and friends first, we turn away and greet someone else first. This would make it a true time of greeting instead of one big sanctuary-wide public display of affection that the solitary get to stand and watch before anyone thinks to turn to them. My friend Fiona has noticed this trend too:

> *Married couples turn to each other first, kissing and/ or hugging, leaving the single standing alone feeling unwelcomed and isolated, until finally they break apart from one another and from their own children to greet others around them.*

I admit I've been guilty of this many times myself, when I've been in church with family and friends. It's an instinct we all have—but there are times when instinct needs to be suppressed for the sake of including the less fortunate.

> *Invite [singles] into your homes. Singles like being around married couples and families. Don't assume, because we don't have kids, that we might not enjoy watching* Tangled *with your kids and you on a Friday night. We also don't always mind getting to be a part of a game night with couples either. Couples are often fun!*—Allison

Yes, it's hard and uncomfortable sometimes. It can be really tough to find common ground. And it's even tougher because there are so many differences, not just between singles and married people but also between one single person and another. The single people in your church come in all shapes and sizes; all ethnicities, genders, and ages; and with all different kinds of life experiences behind them. I don't know the particular single in your pew and I can't speak for that person specifically, but I can tell you that, more than likely, he or she is facing pressures and struggles you may never have even dreamed of. Maybe this person finds it as hard to talk to you as you do to talk to him or her. So maybe you find this person confusing or frustrating; maybe you have no idea how to reach out.

And maybe you're in that position where the singles in your church are all telling you something different. Some want a singles ministry and some don't; some are eager to be set up and some roll their eyes at the idea; some are petitioning to be let out of nursery duty and others are clamoring for more of it. Maybe there are even differences in how they think about marriage—some want it and some don't. If so, that's not surprising. Single people are not controlled by a hive mind. We don't all have one monolithic point of view on every issue—we're a group of diverse people with varying opinions, just like any given group of people. We want different things and we're going to disagree. And that's all right. Issues can be worked out and compromises can be reached. But in order to do that, to even get that process started, the church needs to be willing to make it a priority.

❖   ❖   ❖

If I could take one guess at what the single in your pew might say to you, given the opportunity, I would guess that it's this: *listen*. Please listen. Take the time to ask questions, to let the person answer, to hear without judging or jumping in with canned Christian formulas or buzzwords.

When you hear someone say that singleness is really hard, and you're tempted to retort, "You don't know what 'hard' is!"—stop. Catch yourself. Push away the impulse to correct and judge and win the "who has the more difficult life" contest. Ask what's going on that's hard and be prepared to listen.

Yes, it's possible that you'll hear something so silly you'll need to excuse yourself and go find a quiet place to roll your eyes. That's always a risk in human interaction. But it's also possible you'll hear about someone struggling to pay rent or medical bills on one salary. Or about someone who doesn't think he or she can face coming home to a dark and silent apartment one more time. Or about someone dealing with sexual desires and temptations that are becoming too great to bear. You may have the chance to say something that will strengthen and shore up someone's faith—or you may learn something that will give new life and strength to yours.

If someone mentions having a hard time trying to get a date, you could give them the standard "Have you tried online dating yet?" and then leave it there, secure in the knowledge you've done all you could do by making the suggestion. Or you could listen to the answer and hear how that's going. You could rejoice with them over hopeful prospects or offer support and empathy when they tell you they just don't think they can face one more rejection.

And please don't think you have to wait until everything in your life is perfect before you can make an effort. If you abruptly get called away two sentences into a conversation because your toddler poured juice on the cat, or your five-year-old gave your three-year-old a haircut, or your teenager backed out of the garage without bothering to put the door up first—that's okay. We get it. Any single person with sense (and there are more of those than you might suppose!) recognizes and accepts that we cannot come first in your lives, that some things are more important.

But we would simply ask you this: keep trying. Keep making those imperfect efforts. However short and stilted and interruption-prone they might be, they matter. In fact, the friendships you create this way might end up meaning just as much to you as they do to the single people you're befriending.

Wesley Hill, author of *Spiritual Friendship*, is uniquely situated to reflect on these friendships and our deep need for them. Hill is a same-sex-attracted man who has chosen to live a celibate life because of his Christian faith. In his book, he writes of "the myth of freedom" that has dominated our culture and infiltrated the church, affecting not just single people but families as well.

> One of the characters in Willa Cather's novel *Shadows on the Rock* says, "Only solitary men know the full joys of friendship. Others have their family; but to a solitary and an exile his friends are everything." By the same token, I'd say that only solitary people know the full sorrows of friendship's gradual diminishment in our culture as we maintain our commitment to maximal individual autonomy. I talk regularly with many of these people: men and women who have passed the usual age for marriage and child rearing and who turn to the church, hoping to find a robust vision of committed friendship, only to encounter a looser, more casual form of

social life that seems to say, *We can be friends, so long as it doesn't require too many sacrifices.*

But it's not just single people who are harmed by our commitment to the myth of freedom. Married couples and parents stand to lose as well. Over the last several months, I've had poignant conversations with several friends who are young mothers. They all tell me the same story. When you're at home caring for an infant or a toddler, it can be easy to feel as though your world is contracting, and you're left scrabbling your way along a lightless tunnel by yourself, your only companion a drooling, jabbering creature who can't sympathize with your needs and engage you in meaningful conversation.[11]

Or as my pastor, Johnny Kurcina, put it in a recent sermon:

We [in the church] have elevated the nuclear family, which sounds like we're elevating community. But . . . now we live in a culture of nuclear families that are completely autonomous from everyone else. No one else has a say in my household. Now we have community, the five of us, but no one else has a say. We're people with little commitment to church, to place, to community, to anything. Why? Because as an American, I know it's *my* home, *my* career, *my* money, *my* time. [But] Christianity suggests that we are made for relationships, to be part of a Body—that we are formed in community.[12]

Personally, I consider myself a bit less stringent about these things than Hill and some of the people in that group at my church. At times, understanding the stress and the pressures that so many people are under today, and experiencing my own fair share of them (not to mention being an introvert), I'm okay with a looser, more casual form of social life. I

214

don't feel that I need the kind of community where we all live on top of each other.

Actually, if I were in one, I'd probably start climbing the walls. While I'm not averse to some of the group living arrangements that many singles and married people share (more on that in a moment), I'm not sure I could go as far as, say, promising to check with the church before taking a job in another city. That kind of closeness might override my sense of boundaries—and every person, married or single, needs those.

But however close to our friends or distant from them we may need to be sometimes, we all need that network of people who care about us, who are there when we need them, who remember that we exist. At some level, we need to be part of each other's lives.

Blogger Abigail Dodds describes a few of the single Christian women who had been a blessing to her and her family:

> I found myself telling Joyce about a challenge I was facing in parenting. She responded by saying, "I've never had children, so I don't know if this will be helpful, but here's what I've observed with my nieces and nephews." This surprised me—even more surprising, that she had never been married. I hadn't considered the possibility that the woman eager to take some green moms under her wing would be single. I am thankful she did. . . .
>
> My Aunt Julie has always been an integral part of my life. Her lifelong singleness has been a gift to us. I don't say that to minimize the difficulty of it. Her singleness, coupled with her willingness to love us, warts and all, and take us under her wing, has been a type of auntly mothering that is as precious as it is unique.

When I watch my two-year-old son's face light up at the sight of her, or see the older kids sprint to invade the privacy of her room, I'm thankful.[13]

Micha Boyett, a mother of three active boys, recently wrote about what it's like to have a single friend, Leigh, living with her and her family. An arrangement that began out of convenience has blossomed into something special for both the Boyetts and Leigh. Not only have they been able to help each other with chores and duties, share financial burdens, and enjoy each other's companionship, but everyone has had the chance to learn something.

> Leigh and I are the same age, just with different marital statuses. While I wed in my 20s and had kids at a generically 30-ish time in my life, she has had to navigate *not* leading the typical 30-something mom-life. Surprisingly, one of the most noticeable places this difference comes into play is at church. Over the last year, I've started to notice that the needs of families in the church are louder than the needs of single people. . . .
>
> Single people can feel invisible in the place they most need to be seen. Leigh has helped me see that more clearly. She has helped me understand a little more of what it feels like to be a sideline voice in a community.[14]

For those who truly desire to learn what it means to embrace life in community, to reach out to every member of it—not just the ones who most closely resemble us—that's not a bad place to start.

You don't need to have a single person come and live in your house. You don't even have to live near one. But if you want to learn to love all the members of your church, singles included, with a truly Christlike love, I humbly suggest that, as much as you're able, you do need to start thinking about how and where you can make space for us in your lives.

Love and Serve

My own family history has been something of a theme in this book, and I hope you won't mind if I go back to it one more time, this time in some detail. When I think about strong relationships between married people and single people, and how they can flourish, I think of my great-aunt Mary D'alfonso[15]—even though I never had the opportunity to meet her. Like me, Mary was single, but she was single in a very different time and place.

My parents both grew up in Greenville, Pennsylvania, a tiny town about seventy miles outside of Pittsburgh. It was one of those towns where you not only knew everyone but also were related to almost everyone. Both my parents had big extended families—they couldn't go to school, church, or any of the local hangouts without running into boatloads of cousins. I have twenty-six great-aunts and great-uncles, and that's just counting the ones who are related to me by blood, not by marriage. The vast majority of them stayed right there in Greenville to raise their families.

Of those twenty-six, Mary was one of only three who remained single all her life. The other two were nuns.

I don't know why she was single, whether it was by choice or by circumstance or a little bit of both; I don't know much about her at all. What little I do know came from my parents, Dad's cousin Lucia, and old newspaper articles. I've seen a picture of Mary that once ran in the paper; she was an attractive woman, with dark eyes, curly dark hair, and a nice smile. The accompanying article claimed she was "a loner" and yet "well-known and liked." (As to why her picture and description were in the paper, we'll get to that in a moment.)

Mary was Grandpa Tony's sister, but I don't remember him ever talking about her. He wasn't much of a talker, period. But I do know that they were close. Tony was the oldest boy in a family of six children, and Mary was just a year younger. She was maid of honor at his wedding, even though he married a woman with seven sisters.

Like many of the Italian families in their little Pennsylvania town, the D'alfonsos held firmly to the old Italian traditions they had brought to America with them. Any unmarried children remained at home. My grandfather and his younger brother Tom, who both married late for those times, lived with their parents until they married, and their sister Mary lived at home all her life.

The oldest son in the family was responsible for caring for his parents and any siblings who didn't have families of their own. Both my grandfathers were the oldest sons in their families and knew the heavy burden of this responsibility; both of them were relied on by their parents at an early age and were in many ways like second fathers to their younger siblings. For Grandpa Tony, well into adulthood, this meant things like giving his father rides to and from the factory where he worked and being "on call" whenever one of his parents needed him for anything. It also meant looking out for his sister Mary.

Greenville is a sleepy town nowadays, but back in the 1950s and '60s it was a busy one, and Tony Dalfonzo was probably one of the busiest persons in it. He and his wife (also named

Mary)[16] owned a thriving grocery store, were raising two sons, and were members of at least half the religious, charitable, and civic organizations in town. My grandparents, like most businesspeople of their day, were great believers in businesses being heavily involved in the community, so Grandpa belonged to the Knights of Columbus and the Rotary Club and the Italian Home Club and sat on the boards of the National Association of Retail Grocers and the Pennsylvania Food Merchants Association and I don't know what else.

But with all of that, Tony made time every week to pick up his sister Mary from the train on Friday nights and drive her home, and then pick her up on Sunday nights and drive her back to the train.

If he minded doing it, I'm sure he never said so. My grandfather, as I've mentioned, was a very quiet, very reserved man, but his affections ran deep, and he took good care of those he loved. They probably would have said that acts of service were his love language, had they known about love languages in those days.

But this was later in their lives. Earlier, when my dad was a kid, his aunt Mary worked as a telephone operator right there in Greenville. Another feature of small-town big-family life back in those days: having a relative able to track you at all times, like some sort of powerful and knowledgeable minor deity. Dad couldn't pick up a phone anywhere in town without alerting his aunt to where he was, and if she discerned that he was up to no good, she was more than ready to let him have it.

He was fond of her, nonetheless. When his parents went out of town on business, Dad and his younger brother stayed at their grandmother's house, where Aunt Mary treated them "like royalty." Dad's mouth still waters at the memory of her cooking. She would spend days concocting her version of the famous Italian wedding soup, making the meatballs and the pastina from scratch. And somewhere in between working and cooking, she ran the household and looked after her parents; even after her father was felled by a stroke and required a lot of lifting and hands-on care, she cared for him until his death a year or so later.

Later on Aunt Mary's job was transferred to Bradford, Pennsylvania. It was about two and a half hours from Greenville, but she liked the work and it paid well; she contributed to her family and the upkeep of the house and on top of that was able to collect the china, silver, and crystal she loved. She didn't want to give it up. So she worked there during the week and came home on weekends—hence all those train journeys.

Still later she was transferred to Sharon, much closer to home, and decided it would be easier to drive back and forth. She would have been in her late forties by then, but she had never learned to drive. So her brother Tony taught her and went with her to help her pick out her new car, a little Ford. "She didn't like to drive," Lucia tells me, but she managed the trips all right. Until one night in November 1965.

No one knows exactly what happened that night. The weather was bad, and there was a construction project underway on a causeway that she had to cross. Usually Mary would drive out of her way to avoid the construction, but that night, for some reason, she didn't. It was late, and she may have wanted to get home faster than usual.

All we know for sure is that the morning of November 21, Mary's car was found in ten feet of water in the Shenango River, without her in it.

Both my parents had left home by then—Dad was at college in Ohio, Mom in business school in Minnesota—but both have vivid memories of that awful time, thanks to all they heard about it from those back home. Dad was able to come home from college at Thanksgiving and went out searching with his father a few times. He still remembers feeling the icy wind in his face as their boat poked along every inch of that river . . . with no success.

"My poor father was just heartbroken," Dad remembers. "You couldn't get him off that river." Every day Tony was out there with the rescuers, looking for his sister, while their family and friends did what they could to help out. Not until January was she found, on a bank in Sharpsville, some twelve miles away.

This is a sad, difficult story; you may be wondering why I chose to tell it here. It's because, looking beyond the sadness, I see hope. I see a story—one of so many stories out there—of a woman who lived a good, full life as a single person. She lived a life that, in the eyes of so many people—including many Christians—was a fate worse than death, a life without spouse or children, and she lived it in a time when it was an even more unpopular lifestyle than it is today. And she thrived. She lived her life actively and boldly, making the most of her opportunities. Her death was tragic, but her life was not. She loved, and she was loved, with a love that held on and would not let go even after death.

And there's another reason too. I told you back at the beginning of this book that, being from a large extended family, I've sometimes felt like an inferior person in comparison to all the great-grandmothers and great-aunts and cousins who spent their lives bearing and raising children. I don't discount the blessings I've had in comparison to many of them—like the great blessing of never having to worry about what to eat, for example!—but at times my life has seemed to me small and narrow and incomplete compared to theirs. And I've sometimes wondered what they would have thought of this wayward descendant of theirs.

My grandpa Tony passed away when I was twenty-four. Not a day goes by that I don't miss him. I adored him from the time I was small, and quiet as he was, I knew he adored me too. But sometimes, in the recesses of my mind, I end up lumping him in with all of those other ancestors whom I imagine being bewildered by how my life has turned out. If he had ever thought this far ahead—I don't know whether he did or not—he probably expected great-grandchildren by now, and there have been times when I've wondered if I would have been a disappointment to him.

Then I think of how he loved his single sister, of the time and energy he spent serving her all those years, and I know it's not true. That is a picture of unconditional love that I carry with me, to help me bear up in my toughest moments.

But, you may be thinking, *that was a family relationship; it's not so surprising that such a relationship would have been close and involved selfless service.* True—but isn't that what relationships in the church are supposed to look like? We talk very lightly about our Christian "brothers and sisters," but how many of us truly serve each other like that, even when there are significant differences in status and position? How many of us look past those differences and value each other that highly? How many of us love each other with a love that lasts beyond death, a love that pursues and will not give up?

◆　◆　◆

There are many such relationships in the church, I know—but on the whole, I believe we can do better. I've spent a lot of time in this book critiquing the church, but I've done so because I care deeply about it and I want to see it be what it was made to be: an interdependent group of believers, where "there is neither Jew nor Greek, there is neither slave nor free, there is neither male nor female" (Gal. 3:28), truly worthy of being called the body of Christ. And I might add, with apologies to Paul, "neither married nor single." For all our sakes, and for the sake of the One who calls us, this is what the church should aspire to.

I wouldn't have written this book unless I believed that, with the Holy Spirit's help, the church is capable of this. It is the mission God gave us, after all. But I will have written it for nothing unless it inspires you not just to see the single in your pew in a new light but to act accordingly. The single person who sits next to you on Sundays, or sits under your teaching from the pulpit or in the Sunday school classroom, is not someone else's problem. More than that—he or she is not a problem at all. Instead, that person is, as C. S. Lewis has it:

> Next to the Blessed Sacrament itself, your neighbor is the holiest object presented to your senses.[17]

Something else Lewis wrote, in his essay "First and Second Things," is also relevant here:

> Every preference of a small good to a great, or partial good to a total good, involves the loss of the small or partial good for which the sacrifice is made. . . . You can't get second things by putting them first. You get second things only by putting first things first.[18]

The modern evangelical church has made marriage and family into a first thing. They are good things, of course—as Lewis's rule reminds us, the "second things" in our lives usually do tend to be good things—but they are not the first thing for which the church was created.

But we have lost sight of this. We thought we could improve on our witness by concentrating on happy family life, getting everyone married off before they had a chance to engage in sexual sin, holding up model marriages and children for the world to admire and emulate. Instead, as a slew of statistics and articles shows us, not to mention our own personal experiences, we have increasing divorce rates, children who grow up and walk away from the faith, and, as this book has attempted to show, single Christians who often feel alone and isolated in the middle of a church crowd. We sacrificed our smaller good by exalting it too highly, and in the process we lost our focus on Christ—who taught us to concentrate first and foremost not on filling the church with model families but on seeking out the lost and lonely, sharing His love with them, and loving them and each other as He does.

"By this all will know that you are My disciples, if you have love for one another" (John 13:35). I quoted that verse once before, but as this book draws to a close, it bears repeating. This love that reflects the love of God is our "first thing," the thing that distinguishes us, the thing that we have to offer the world. Love that knows no barriers and no boundaries. Love that reaches out even to the singles in your church.

EPILOGUE
FOOD FOR THOUGHT

If you're a married Christian and you've read this far—first of all, thank you. I'm very grateful that you were interested enough to find out more about the experiences and the needs of the single people at your church and that you took the time to follow through on that interest.

Maybe now you're asking yourself where to go from here. What are the next steps to take to reach out to singles and integrate them fully into the life of the church? Or, to put it on a more personal and practical level, how can you connect with your single brother or sister in Christ in ways that will bless and build up both of you?

I've drawn on some of the themes in this book to compile what I hope will be a handy and helpful list for you to rely on in the days and weeks to come. And I've gone the alliterative route to help you remember it better.

- **Look.** Train yourself to see—really see—the single people in your church. Don't ignore them as you make a beeline to talk to others who are just like you; don't glance past them at the family walking or sitting just behind them. Make it a point to look for them and look at them. Practice this at every church service, every Bible study, every worship team or choir practice, every congregational meeting. Pay attention. The more you train your eyes to notice and your mind to recognize that they're among you and they matter, the more they *will* matter to you.

- **Listen.** Don't just stop at looking, of course—that would be pointless and a little creepy. When you notice a single person at church, make the effort to go over and talk. *And* to listen. You'd think the two—talking and listening—would automatically go together, but the truth is they don't always. Ask questions, and really listen to and consider the answers. Remember that people can tell whether you're talking just to hear yourself talk or you really want to also hear what they're saying. In an earlier chapter I mentioned Bob and Nancy, who were friends and mentors to me at my former church. I remember one time when Bob simply said to me, "How are you?" and I froze, lost for words, because I honestly could not remember the last time someone had said that to me in that way—a way that indicated they actually cared how I was. Be that person. Be the person who asks, and cares, and listens.

- **Learn.** This is, of course, very closely related to listening, but it goes deeper. To learn, you have to listen with your defenses down, or at least a little lowered. You have to be willing to acknowledge that there are people in your church who are different from you, who have experiences and memories and points of view that may be very different from yours—and that this is okay. We may pay lip service to that idea, but few of us are really comfortable with it when confronted with it head-on. You may feel an overwhelming urge to correct, to override, to corral the conversation and bring it back to where you feel safe. Don't do it. Resist the urge to react. Even if you feel that you're hearing something wrong or unfair or naïve—and perhaps you are—practice the art of restraint. You can make your points or your arguments another time, perhaps after you've gotten to know the person better and established an actual relationship. And bear in mind that, on issues of singleness and marriage, yours is most likely the mainstream point of view in your church. The single person has already heard your point of view from the pulpit and from the congregation and from all over the church, but has anyone heard his or hers? Maybe you'll be the first. Don't squander the opportunity.

- **Love.** This is where you take what you've learned and put it into practice, both by reaching out in friendship to the single Christians around you and by helping the church incorporate their ideas and meet their needs. This is how you demonstrate the love of Christ for your single brothers and sisters in the church.

I'm not saying it's easy; it's not. It takes time and effort and genuine concern for their welfare. Why make that effort? Because of the words of Jesus in Matthew 25:40: "Assuredly, I say to you, inasmuch as you did it to one of the least of these My brethren, you did it to Me."

As I've explained in this book, single people in church too often have been relegated to the role of "the least of these." You can start to change that. In doing so, you can paint a truer picture of Christ, not just for single people but for the church and the world.

NOTES

Introduction

1. "Daisy," comment on "Singles: Excluded and Dismissed," *Wartburg Watch*, August 2, 2013, http://thewartburgwatch.com/2013/08/02/singles-excluded-and -dismissed/#comment-109163.

2. Gina Dalfonzo, "Abstinence Is Not Rocket Science," *Christianity Today*, September 15, 2011, http://www.christianitytoday.com/ct/2011/septemberweb-only/abstinence-not-rocket-science.html.

3. W. Bradford Wilcox, interviewed by Kathryn Jean Lopez, "Does 'The Back-Up Plan' Work?" *National Review Online*, June 19, 2010, http://www.national review.com/corner/232162/does-back-plan-work-kathryn-jean-lopez.

Section 1 Stigmas, Stereotypes, and Shame

1. Mei Fong, interviewed in "How China's One-Child Policy Led to Forced Abortions, 30 Million Bachelors," *Fresh Air*, NPR, February 1, 2016, http://www .npr.org/2016/02/01/465124337/how-chinas-one-child-policy-led-to-forced -abortions-30-million-bachelors.

2. Mark Driscoll, "Single Like Jesus," quoted in "Mark Driscoll Pastor of Mars Hill—Views on Singleness," *Christian Pundit*, September 21, 2012, https:// christianpundit.wordpress.com/2012/09/21/mark-driscoll-pastor-of-mars-hill-views-on-singleness/. Full sermon available on YouTube, https://www.youtube .com/watch?v=YhFyPQjarSU (posted February 13, 2013).

Chapter 1 Singles as Problems

1. As quoted in Camerin Courtney, "Is Singleness a Sin?" *Christianity Today*, August 11, 2004, http://www.crosswalk.com/11621125/.

2. Ibid.

3. Dr. R. Albert Mohler Jr., "Looking Back at 'The Mystery of Marriage'—Part Two," AlbertMohler.com, August 20, 2004, http://www.albertmohler.com/2004/08/20/looking-back-at-the-mystery-of-marriage-part-two/.
4. Courtney, "Is Singleness a Sin?"
5. Candice Watters, *Get Married: What Women Can Do to Help It Happen* (Chicago: Moody, 2008), 13–14.
6. Eric Reed, "Six Reasons Young People Leave the Church," *Leadership Journal*, Winter 2012, http://www.christianitytoday.com/le/2012/winter/youngleavechurch.html.
7. Debbie Maken, *Getting Serious about Getting Married: Rethinking the Gift of Singleness* (Wheaton: Crossway, 2006), 17.

Chapter 2 Singles as Pariahs

1. Kate Hurley, *Cupid Is a Procrastinator: Making Sense of the Unexpected Single Life* (Eugene, OR: Harvest House, 2013), 101.
2. Jeremy Myers, "Is Divorce the Unforgivable Sin?" *Redeeming God*, accessed December 14, 2016, https://redeeminggod.com/divorce-unforgivable-sin/.
3. Lisa Anderson, *The Dating Manifesto: A Drama-Free Plan for Pursuing Marriage with Purpose* (Colorado Springs: David C. Cook, 2015), 212–13.
4. Lydia Brownback, "Fine China Is for Single Women Too," excerpt from *Fine China Is for Single Women Too* (Phillipsburg, NJ: P&R, 2003), http://www.cbn.com/family/DatingSingles/finechina.aspx.
5. Alec Guinness, *Blessings in Disguise* (New York: Warner Books, 1985), 222.
6. Ibid., 224.
7. Anderson, *Dating Manifesto*, 181.
8. C. S. Lewis, *The Screwtape Letters* (New York: Collier Books, 1982), 39.
9. Amanda McCracken, "When True Love Keeps Waiting," *Christianity Today*, April 1, 2015, http://www.christianitytoday.com/women/2015/april/when-true-love-keeps-waiting.html.
10. Tyler Charles, "The Secret Sexual Revolution," *Relevant*, February 20, 2012, http://www.relevantmagazine.com/life/relationship/features/28337-the-secret-sexual-revolution#JJ5I7FH7BBtWJI07.99. The study referenced can be found at http://www.thenationalcampaign.org/national-data/default.aspx.
11. See my article "Porn and the Singleness Panic," *Christianity Today*, November 14, 2014, http://www.christianitytoday.com/women/2014/november/porn-and-singleness-panic.html?paging=off.
12. Roberto A. Ferdman, "There Are Only Three Ways to Meet Anyone Anymore," *Wonkblog*, March 8, 2016, https://www.washingtonpost.com/news/wonk/wp/2016/03/08/how-much-life-has-changed-in-one-incredible-chart-about-dating/?wpisrc=nl_rainbow.
13. Anthony Esolen, "Who Will Rescue the Lost Sheep of the Lonely Revolution?" *Crisis*, November 6, 2014, http://www.crisismagazine.com/2014/will-rescue-lost-sheep-lonely-revolution. Emphasis in original. Note: I'm not altogether happy about Esolen's references to girls and "men," which make it sound as though these single people can never reach maturity without marriage, and I don't mean to give the impression I endorse that view. But the rest of what he says here is so good that I believe the passage is well worth including, despite that flaw.
14. McCracken, "When True Love Keeps Waiting."

Chapter 3 Singles as Projects

1. This interview was conducted a few years ago. As you may know, Mark Driscoll's church in Seattle closed down after a series of scandals. He now preaches in Phoenix, Arizona.
2. Gina Dalfonzo, "The Good Christian Girl: A Fable," *Christianity Today*, July 19, 2010, http://www.christianitytoday.com/ct/2010/julyweb-only/good -christian-girl-fable.html.
3. Jon Acuff, "Surviving Church as a Single," *Stuff Christians Like*, June 1, 2009, http://stuffchristianslike.net/2009/06/01/550-surviving-church-as-a-single/.
4. Cindy Johnson, *Who's Picking Me Up from the Airport? and Other Questions Single Girls Ask* (Grand Rapids: Zondervan, 2015), 22–23.
5. Ibid.
6. From an unpublished manuscript by Joanna Holman. Used with permission.
7. Johnson, *Who's Picking Me Up from the Airport?*, 22.
8. Candice Watters, "Should I Pay More Attention to My Appearance?" *Boundless*, November 27, 2006, http://www.boundless.org/advice/2006/should-i-pay -more-attention-to-my-appearance.
9. Jon Birger, *Date-Onomics: How Dating Became a Lopsided Numbers Game* (New York: Workman Publishing, 2015), 9.
10. Ibid., 17.
11. Clare Clark, *We That Are Left* (New York: Houghton Mifflin Harcourt, 2015), 268–69.

Chapter 4 Singles as People

1. Anna Davies, interview with Meghann Foyle, "I Want All of the Perks of Maternity Leave—without Having Any Kids," *New York Post*, April 28, 2016, http://nypost.com/2016/04/28/i-want-all-the-perks-of-maternity-leave-without -having-any-kids/.
2. Conversation quoted with permission.
3. Jennifer Fulwiler, interviewed by Caryn Rivadeneira, "How Does She Do It?: 12 Life Questions for Radio Host Jennifer Fulwiler," *For Her*, August 16, 2016, http://forher.aleteia.org/articles/how-does-she-do-it-jennifer-fulwiler -work-life-balance-tricks/.
4. "Kelly," comment, Lindsey Nobles, "Church and the Single Girl," LindseyNobles.com, November 30, 2015, http://www.lindseynobles.com/2015/11/church-and -the-single-girl/.
5. Ibid.

Section 2 How We Got Here

1. C. S. Lewis, *The Abolition of Man* (New York, HarporOne, 2015), 26.
2. Annie F. Downs, *Let's All Be Brave* (Grand Rapids: Zondervan, 2014), 167.

Chapter 5 The Man in the Hat

1. Tim Challies, "The Bestsellers: I Kissed Dating Goodbye," Challies.com, March 30, 2014, http://www.challies.com/articles/the-bestsellers-i-kissed-dating -goodbye.

2. "David B.," "I Kissed Dating Good-Bye," *Per Christum*, August 2, 2008, http://blog.ancient-future.net/2008/08/02/i-kissed-dating-good-bye/.

3. Tim Holland, "I Kissed Dating Goodbye, Where Did It Go?" *Relevant*, June 3, 2009, http://www.relevantmagazine.com/life/relationship/features/17083-i-kissed-dating-goodbye-but-where-did-it-go#3lBhdTCskhpi6qQb.99.

4. See C. S. Lewis, *An Experiment in Criticism* (Cambridge: Cambridge University Press, 2000), 104–6.

5. See David Crank, "Approaches to Courtship/Betrothal," *Unless the Lord*, March/April 2003, http://www.unlessthelordmagazine.com/articles/Courtship%20Approaches.htm, for a brief but helpful explanation of the connections among Gothard, Harris, and other teachers on courtship. See also "Steve240," "Did Joshua Harris 'Forget' His Own Church's History with Courtship/Groups?" at his blog *I Kissed Dating Goodbye—Wisdom or Foolishness*, February 25, 2008, http://ikdg.wordpress.com/2008/02/25/did-joshua-harris-forget-his-own-churchs-history-with-courtshipgroups/.

6. These days, ironically, Gothard is also known for stepping down from his ministry in the face of multiple allegations of sexual harassment by women who used to work for him. See Sarah Pulliam Bailey, "Conservative Leader Bill Gothard Resigns Following Abuse Allegations," *Washington Post*, March 7, 2014, http://www.washingtonpost.com/national/religion/conservative-leader-bill-gothard-resigns-following-abuse-allegations/2014/03/07/0381aa94-a624-11e3-b865-38b254d92063_story.html/.

7. Joshua Harris, *I Kissed Dating Goodbye*, updated ed. (Colorado Springs: Multnomah, 2003), 14.

8. Patchin's article, originally published at *Boundless*, is no longer available there but has been archived under the title "In Defense of a Virginal Heart" at http://www.angelfire.com/id/princesspeanut/waitingforlove/article.html.

9. Sam Torode, foreword to *I Kissed Dating Goodbye*, 8.

10. Mark Oppenheimer, "An Evolving View of Natural Family Planning," *New York Times*, July 8, 2011, http://www.nytimes.com/2011/07/09/us/09beliefs.html?_r=1&.

11. Joshua Harris, *Boy Meets Girl: Say Hello to Courtship* (Colorado Springs: Multnomah, 2005), 127.

12. Ibid., 128.

13. Ibid.

14. Both Kerrin and Megan have written online about what happened (see "Kerrin's Story, part i," *SGM Survivors*, June 16, 2011, http://www.sgmsurvivors.com/2011/06/16/kerrins-story-part-i/; "Kerrin's Story, part ii," *SGM Survivors*, June 21, 2011, http://www.sgmsurvivors.com/2011/06/21/kerrins-story-part-ii/; and "Megan's Response," *SGM Survivors*, June 30, 2011, http://www.sgmsurvivors.com/2011/06/30/megans-response/. Neither they nor Joshua Harris give the date of their marriage, so "eleven or twelve years" is as close as I can come. See also "Victoria," "Another Look at Kissing Dating Goodbye," *Be More Heart, and Less Attack*, February 4, 2016, http://moreheartlessattack.blogspot.com/2015/02/another-look-at-kissing-dating-goodbye.html.

15. Thomas Umstattd Jr., "Why Courtship Is Fundamentally Flawed," ThomasUmstattd.com, August 12, 2014, http://www.thomasumstattd.com/2014/08/courtship-fundamentally-flawed/.

16. Also, as he revealed much later while his church was in the throes of a sexual abuse scandal, Harris himself tragically had been a victim of sexual abuse at a young age. (See Michelle Van Loon, "He Kissed the Secret of His Childhood Sexual Abuse Goodbye," Pilgrim's Road Trip, *Patheos*, May 24, 2013, http://www.patheos.com/blogs/pilgrimsroadtrip/2013/05/he-kissed-the-secret-of-his-childhood-sexual-abuse-goodbye/.) We can't know how much this terrible crime committed against him in his childhood may have affected Harris's thinking on relationships. It would have affected *anyone's* thinking.

Chapter 6 Courtship Crazy

1. Harris, *Boy Meets Girl*, 54–70.
2. Eric and Leslie Ludy, *When God Writes Your Love Story*, expanded ed. (Colorado Springs: Multnomah, 2009), 89.
3. Ibid., 5.
4. Ibid., 54.
5. Mary Kassian, *Girls Gone Wise in a World Gone Wild* (Chicago: Moody, 2010), 119–20.
6. Ibid., 134.
7. Elisabeth Elliot, *Passion and Purity* (Grand Rapids: Revell, 2003), 111.
8. Watters, *Get Married*, 111–19.
9. Ibid.

Chapter 7 Pressure and Paralysis

1. Joshua Harris, "Courtship Shmourtship," sermon at Covenant Life Church, Gaithersburg, MD, November 20, 2005, http://www.covlife.org/resources/2671357-Courtship_Shmourtship.
2. Joshua Harris, interview with Rachel Martin, "Former Evangelical Pastor Rethinks His Approach to Courtship," *Weekend Edition Sunday*, NPR, July 10, 2016, http://www.npr.org/2016/07/10/485432485/former-evangelical-pastor-rethinks-his-approach-to-courtship.
3. Darcy Anne Saffer, "How the Teachings of Emotional Purity and Courtship Damage Healthy Relationships," *Darcy's Heart-Stirrings*, January 18, 2011, http://darcysheartstirrings.blogspot.com/2011/01/how-teachings-of-emotional-purity-and.html.
4. Ross Boone, "Give Us Guys a Break," *Boundless*, July 27, 2016, http://www.boundless.org/blog/give-us-guys-break/.
5. Susan Olasky, "Christian Boy Meets Christian Girl," *World*, May 20, 2011, http://www.worldmag.com/2011/05/christian_boy_meets_christian_girl.
6. Oppenheimer, "An Evolving View of Natural Family Planning."
7. Umstattd, "Why Courtship Is Fundamentally Flawed."
8. Lauren Wilford, "First Love, Last Love: Courtship Culture and the Teen Cancer Romance," *Christianity Today*, February 14, 2016, http://www.christianitytoday.com/ct/2016/february-web-only/first-love-last-love-courtship-culture-and-teen-cancer-roma.html?share=KABMU1VlhStn5l4yRiL4IAg0yJHC1xIF.

Chapter 8 Friendly Fire

1. Conversation quoted with permission.

2. There are those, most likely, who feel this is exactly what I'm doing with this book! But that's not what I'm trying to do. While I want to help hold the church accountable for the mistakes it's made in this area, I'm not saying it's wholly to blame for the rise in singleness and the problems of singles. There are many factors at work here; the church is only one of them.

3. John Piper, "Should Women Be Police Officers?" *Desiring God*, August 13, 2015, http://www.desiringgod.org/interviews/should-women-be-police-officers.

4. Bianca Olthoff, "Dating: A Male Point of View . . ." BiancaOlthoff.com, January 2013, http://www.biancaolthoff.com/dating-a-male-point-of-view/. Emphasis in original.

5. Dianna E. Anderson, *Damaged Goods: New Perspectives on Christian Purity* (New York: Jericho Books, 2015), 163. I reviewed this book here: http://www.christianitytoday.com/women/2015/march/choose-your-own-sexual-ethics-adventure.html?start=1.

6. See, for example, Eliel Cruz, "11 Reasons Christianity Needs Feminism," *Huffington Post*, May 21, 2014, http://www.huffingtonpost.com/eliel-cruz/11-reasons-christianity-n_b_5365210.html.

7. David Zahl, "Are You Man Enough? When Virile Was a Compliment," *Mockingbird*, May 25, 2016, http://www.mbird.com/2016/05/when-virile-was-a-compliment/.

8. Danielle Paquette, "The Stark Difference between Millennial Men and Their Dads," *Washington Post*, May 26, 2016, https://www.washingtonpost.com/news/wonk/wp/2016/05/26/the-stark-difference-between-millennial-men-and-their-dads/?postshare=2661464282895478&tid=ss_tw.

9. Ibid.

10. Joylon Jenkins, "The Men Who Are Fighting against 'Female Supremacy,'" *Out of the Ordinary*, BBC Radio 4, March 14, 2016, http://www.bbc.co.uk/programmes/p03mnvzb.

11. Suzanne Venker, "Why Men Won't Marry You," FoxNews.com, May 1, 2015, http://www.foxnews.com/opinion/2015/05/01/why-men-wont-marry.html.

12. W. Bradford Wilcox, "The Divorce Revolution Has Bred an Army of Woman Haters," *Federalist*, May 19, 2016, http://thefederalist.com/2016/05/19/the-divorce-revolution-has-bred-an-army-of-woman-haters/.

13. Ibid.

14. Quoted by Peter Kirk in "Driscoll: Single Men 'Cannot Fully Reflect God,'" *Gentle Wisdom*, November 20, 2007, http://www.gentlewisdom.org/306/driscoll-single-men-cannot-fully-reflect-god/.

15. See, for example, Elizabeth Bruenig, "The Failure of Macho Christianity," *New Republic*, February 24, 2015, https://newrepublic.com/article/121138/mark-driscoll-and-macho-christianity.

16. See Richard Beck, "Thoughts on Mark Driscoll . . . While I'm Knitting," *Experimental Theology*, February 14, 2009, http://experimentaltheology.blogspot.com/2009/02/thoughts-on-mark-driscoll-while-im.html.

17. Bruenig, "Failure of Macho Christianity."

18. John 13:35.

Chapter 9 Two Stories

1. Robin Jones Gunn, *Surprise Endings,* in *The Christy Miller Collection*, vol. 2 (Colorado Springs: Multnomah, 2006), 68–69.

2. Ibid., 147.

3. Robin Jones Gunn, *A Heart Full of Hope* (Bloomington, MN: Bethany, 1999), 131.

4. Dorothy L. Sayers, *Gaudy Night* (New York: HarperPerennial, 1993), 465.

5. Dorothy L. Sayers, *Have His Carcase* (New York: Harper & Row, 1960), 35.

6. Mark 7:13.

Chapter 10 Rethinking Our Values

1. Rachel McMillan, "Is Homemaking the Church's New Idol?" BreakPoint. org, July 8, 2014, http://www.breakpoint.org/component/blog/entry/12/25646.

2. Rebecca Traister, "The Single American Woman," *New York*, February 22, 2016, http://nymag.com/thecut/2016/02/political-power-single-women-c-v-r.html. Adapted from Traister's book *All the Single Ladies: Unmarried Women and the Rise of an Independent Nation* (New York: Simon & Schuster, 2016).

3. Anika Smith, "Don't Underestimate Single Women Voters," *Christianity Today*, March 4, 2016, http://www.christianitytoday.com/women/2016/march /dont-underestimate-single-women-voters.html.

4. Ibid.

5. Dena Johnson, "3 Beautiful Truths Every Divorced Christian Needs to Know," *Crosswalk*, March 13, 2015, http://www.crosswalk.com/family/marriage /divorce-and-remarriage/3-beautiful-truths-every-divorced-christian-needs-to -know.html.

6. Chris Bohjalian, *The Guest Room* (New York: Doubleday, 2016), 40–41.

7. Ibid., 144.

8. For more on *The Guest Room*, see my review: "The Party's Over," Break-Point.org, February 29, 2016, https://www.breakpoint.org/features-columns /articles/entry/12/28939.

9. Christena Cleveland, "Singled Out: How Churches Can Embrace Unmarried Adults," ChristenaCleveland.com, December 2, 2013, http://www.christena cleveland.com/blogarchive/2013/12/singled-out?rq=Singled%20Out. Emphasis in original.

10. Saleama A. Ruvalcaba, "The Church That Cliques," *Gifted for Leadership*, June 22, 2015, http://www.christianitytoday.com/gifted-for-leadership/2015/june /church-that-cliques.html.

11. "Symphony of Illumination," *How I Met Your Mother*, season 7, episode 12. I was able to get the exact wording from "How I Met Your Mother Transcripts," http://transcripts.foreverdreaming.org/viewforum.php?f=177. (Yes, there are websites that carry complete sets of transcripts from television shows. The internet is a wonderful place.)

12. Ibid.

13. Ibid.

14. Forgive me for mixing together my fictional scenarios. As you may have gathered by now, sometimes I think better in fictional terms!

15. Emilie Le Beau, "The Politics of Parking an Adult at the Kids' Table," *Seattle Times*, November 18, 2006, http://community.seattletimes.nwsource.com /archive/?date=20061118&slug=kidstable18.

16. Lauren Levine, "Why Are Single People Stuck at Life's Kids' Table?" *Thought Catalog*, September 29, 2015, http://thoughtcatalog.com/lauren-levine/2015/09/why-are-single-people-stuck-at-lifes-kids-table/.

17. Janice Shaw Crouse, "The Crisis of Modern Male Immaturity," *American Thinker*, March 25, 2011, http://www.americanthinker.com/articles/2011/03/the_crisis_of_modern_male_imma.html.

18. Dr. Henry Cloud and Dr. John Townsend, *Boundaries* (Grand Rapids: Zondervan, 1992), 32.

19. Dale S. Kuehne, *Sex and the iWorld: Rethinking Relationship beyond an Age of Individualism* (Grand Rapids: Baker Academic, 2009), 127.

20. Alastair J. Minnis, *Chaucer and Pagan Antiquity* (Cambridge: D. S. Brewer, 1982), 131.

21. Dawn Eden, *The Thrill of the Chaste: Finding Fulfillment while Keeping Your Clothes On*, Catholic edition (Notre Dame: Ave Maria, 2015), 55.

22. Ibid.

23. C. S. Lewis, *The Great Divorce* (New York: Collier Books, 1946), 82–83.

Chapter 11 What the Church Gets Right

1. C. S. Lewis, *Mere Christianity* (New York: Macmillan, 1952), 144.

2. I can think of just one exception: Benedict Cumberbatch's Sherlock Holmes in the BBC/PBS series *Sherlock*. But he sees himself as "asexual," which makes it more acceptable—anything you can put a label on automatically becomes more acceptable. Besides, well, it's Benedict Cumberbatch. 'Nuff said.

3. Charles Dickens, *Little Dorrit* (New York: Penguin, 1985), 206–7.

4. See Charles Dickens, "Letter to the Rev. David Macrae," in *The Selected Letters of Charles Dickens*, ed. Jenny Hartley (Oxford: Oxford University Press, 2012), 364.

5. Lisa De Pasquale, "Conservatives' Unexpected Advice on Love and Marriage," Medium.com, February 13, 2016, https://medium.com/@LisaDeP/conservatives-unexpected-advice-on-love-and-marriage-7e0d1b68657#.e6rnotjtp.

6. Dr. Yvonne Kristin Fulbright, "FOXSexpert: Sex on the First Date: Do or Don't?" FoxNews.com, October 13, 2008, http://www.foxnews.com/story/2008/10/13/foxsexpert-sex-on-first-date-do-or-dont.html.

7. Patrick Hruby, "Estranged Bedfellows: Liberals, Conservatives also Split on Sex, Romance," *Washington Times,* February 6, 2012, http://www.washingtontimes.com/news/2012/feb/6/survey-liberals-conservatives-split-sex-romance/.

8. Joel J. Miller, "The Trouble with Me-and-Jesus Christianity," *Ancient Faith Ministries*, February 8, 2016, https://blogs.ancientfaith.com/joeljmiller/me-and-jesus-christianity/.

Chapter 12 We Need Each Other

1. Nancy Jo Sales, "Tinder and the Dawn of the 'Dating Apocalypse,'" *Vanity Fair*, September 2015, http://www.vanityfair.com/culture/2015/08/tinder-hook-up-culture-end-of-dating.

2. Leah Fessler, "Most Women Don't Enjoy Hookup Culture—So Why Do We Force Ourselves to Participate?" *Quartz*, May 17, 2016, http://qz.com/685852/hookup-culture/.

3. Ibid.

4. Miriam Neff, "The Widow's Might," *Christianity Today*, January 18, 2008, http://www.christianitytoday.com/ct/2008/january/26.42.html.

5. Gaye Clark, "9 Things You Need to Know about Widows," *The Gospel Coalition*, January 16, 2015, https://www.thegospelcoalition.org/article/9-things -you-need-to-know-about-widows.

6. Sayers, *Gaudy Night*, 180.

7. Stanley Hauerwas, interviewed by Peter Mommsen, "Why Community Is Dangerous," *Plough*, March 4, 2016, http://www.plough.com/en/topics/com munity/church-community/why-community-is-dangerous.

8. Edith Wharton, *The House of Mirth*, in *Three Novels of New York* (New York: Penguin, 2012), 205.

9. Hauerwas, "Why Community Is Dangerous."

10. Erik Eckholm, "Unmarried Pastor, Seeking a Job, Sees Bias," *New York Times*, March 21, 2011, http://www.nytimes.com/2011/03/22/us/22pastor.html ?_r=2.

11. Wesley J. Hill, *Spiritual Friendship: Finding Love in the Church as a Celibate Gay Christian* (Grand Rapids: Brazos Press, 2015), 14–15.

12. John Kurcina, "The Path," sermon at Christ Church Vienna, Vienna, VA, May 29, 2016, http://www.christchurchvienna.com/sermons/2016/05/the-path/.

13. Abigail Dodds, "Married Moms Need Single Women," *Desiring God*, July 27, 2016, http://www.desiringgod.org/articles/married-moms-need-single-women.

14. Micha Boyett, "You, Me, and Leigh," *For Her*, May 13, 2016, http://forher .aleteia.org/articles/joys-of-single-married-friendship/.

15. The original spelling of the name. My grandfather chose to use a differ- ent spelling for some reason (no one seems to remember why anymore), but his parents and siblings stuck with the old spelling.

16. In those days, if you were Catholic, there were usually more Marys in your family than there are in the New Testament.

17. C. S. Lewis, "The Weight of Glory," in *The Weight of Glory and Other Addresses* (New York: Touchstone, 1980), 40.

18. C. S. Lewis, "First and Second Things," in *God in the Dock: Essays on Theology and Ethics* (Grand Rapids: Eerdmans, 1994), 280. Quoted by Justin Taylor in "The First Things First Principle," *Between Two Worlds*, July 28, 2010, https://blogs.thegospelcoalition.org/justintaylor/2010/07/28/the-first-things-first -principle/.

Gina Dalfonzo is the editor of BreakPoint.org (website of the Colson Center) as well as an occasional writer for BreakPoint Radio. She is also editor of *Dickensblog* and a columnist at *Christ & Pop Culture*. Her writing has been published in the *Atlantic*, *Christianity Today*, *First Things*, *National Review*, the *Weekly Standard*, *Guideposts*, *Aleteia*, the *Stream*, and *OnFaith*, among others. She earned her BA in English from Messiah College and her MA, also in English, from George Mason University. Dalfonzo lives in Springfield, Virginia.

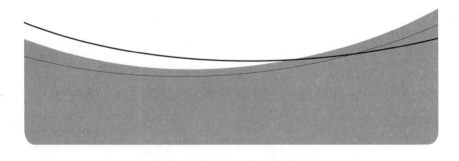